Outdoors in Arizona
A Guide to Fishing and Hunting

ARIZONA
HIGHWAYS BOOK

Text by
Bob Hirsch

Illustrations by
Larry Toschik

Photography by
Arizona Highways Contributors

The bighorn sheep is master of his terrain and walks paths that even the most diligent hunter sometimes cannot follow. James Tallon

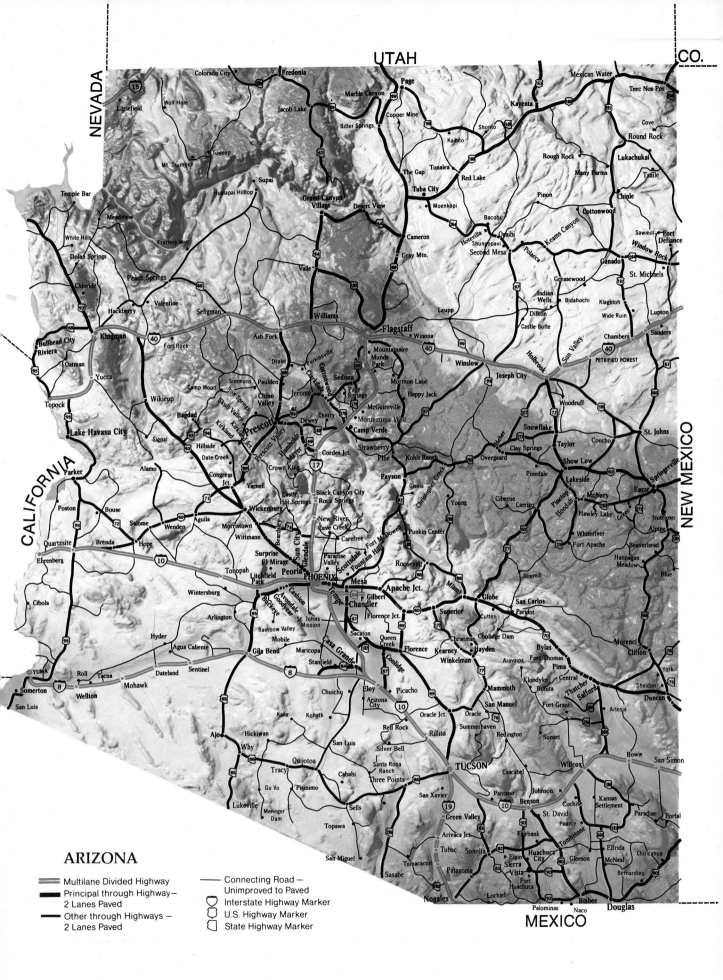

ARIZONA

Legend:
- ══ Multilane Divided Highway
- ━ Principal through Highway— 2 Lanes Paved
- ━ Other through Highways — 2 Lanes Paved
- ─ Connecting Road — Unimproved to Paved
- ⬡ Interstate Highway Marker
- ◯ U.S. Highway Marker
- ⬡ State Highway Marker

NEVADA

UTAH

CO.

CALIFORNIA

NEW MEXICO

MEXICO

3

Regional Map

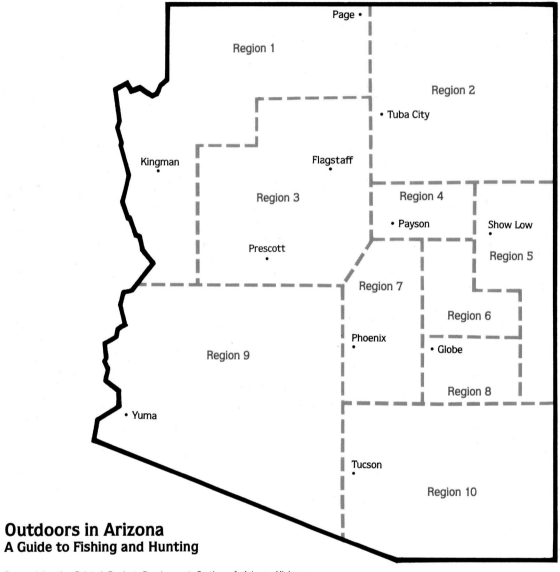

Page •

Region 1

Region 2

• Tuba City

Kingman

Flagstaff

Region 3

Region 4

• Payson

Show Low

Prescott

Region 5

Region 7

Region 6

Phoenix

• Globe

Region 9

Region 8

• Yuma

Tucson

Region 10

Outdoors in Arizona
A Guide to Fishing and Hunting

Prepared by the Related Product Development Section of *Arizona Highways Magazine*, a monthly publication of the Arizona Department of Transportation. Hugh Harelson, Publisher; Wesley Holden, Managing Editor, Related Product Development.

J. PETER MORTIMER — Editor
JAMES R. METCALF — Design and Production
MERRILL WINDSOR — Associate Editor

Library of Congress Catalog Number 85-72179
ISBN 0-916179-05-2

Printed in Japan.

For readers' convenience, Outdoors in Arizona: A Guide to Fishing and Hunting *is organized by geographical regions as indicated above. For this contents map, regional boundaries have been approximated and irregularities squared off. A more precise regional map appears within each chapter.*

The wildlife illustrations appearing on pages 20-21, 36-37, 52-53, 74-75, 132-133, 180, and 186-187 were specially commissioned for this book. The paintings on pages 92-93, 114-115, 148-149, 162-163, and 177 are reproduced by courtesy of Petersen Prints.

Contents

Outdoors in the greatest outdoor state

Someplace in Arizona, every day of the year, the weather is good, the fishing is fine, and some hunting season is under way. This full menu of outdoor activities is unique; nowhere else in the nation does this combination of weather, resources, and opportunity interact in quite the same way.

Fishing and hunting are generally far down the list of reasons people move here. In fact, many give away their fishing tackle and guns, their boats, and their gun dogs, believing they'll have no use for them in their new home. But check the parking lot any Friday at Motorola or IBM or Hughes or Digital. You'll see pickups and campers and mini-motorhomes, all packed and ready to head for the hills when the workday ends. They'll scatter in all directions, these outdoor fans, and they'll do it every week of the year, a testament to the diversity our state has to offer.

In May or June, that Friday afternoon destination might be the Black River and its smallmouth bass. The lonesome stream winds through some of the wildest country in the state and it takes a four-wheel-drive vehicle just to get close enough to walk in; from there on it is backpacking, with only bass, bears, and rattlesnakes for company.

In spring and summer, chances are very good the Arizona angler will choose one of the super reservoirs along the Colorado or Salt rivers, man-made lakes so popular that Arizona ranks close to the top nationally in per capita boat ownership. Powell, Mead, Havasu, Roosevelt, and the rest offer good fishing for more than twenty species of fish. Not bad for a desert state that had just one permanent lake (Stoneman) and two species of game fish (*Salmo apache* and *Salmo gila*) when the first Europeans arrived!

There are small lakes, too, tiny patches of blue scattered in the pines and aspen of the high country, plus dozens of ponds developed for livestock watering that now hold bass, catfish, bluegills, and other warm water dwellers.

It's rather fashionable these days to decry man's stewardship of our natural resources. But when it comes to fishing — at least in Arizona — things have never been better. We have more water, more kinds of fish, and more fish available to catch than ever before. For Arizona anglers, the good old days are right now!

And those newcomers who sold their guns and gear made a big mistake. The rich hunting heritage of the West con-

tinues. There are complex rules and regulations now that reflect the impact of the increasing human population and the resulting loss of wildlife habitat, but the game roster contains a great variety of birds and animals. Hunting for big game species, especially, is strictly controlled and leans toward the conservative.

Seasons and permit numbers are normally structured to crop the annual increase, thus keeping game populations in balance with available habitat and food supplies. Seasons for many of the small game species are long and bag limits are generous, as acknowledgement that hunting has no significant effect on overall populations of quail, rabbits, and the like. Their numbers fluctuate dramatically, usually depending on whether the right amount of rain arrives at the right time of year to assure abundant food and cover.

Fishing and hunting in Arizona revolve around one exciting central fact — opportunity. We don't have as many walleye as Minnesota, for example; Montana has more miles of trout streams, and Alabama can brag about more turkeys. Let other states make their claims to fame; we can counter with an amazing variety of fish and wildlife species in magni-

ficent surroundings that include everything from desert to sub-alpine habitat. Now add good weather and the chance to enjoy the outdoors every day of the year, and it's easy to see why cactus country outdoor fans are so anxious to get out of those parking lots on Friday afternoons.

So welcome to Arizona fishing and hunting. Welcome to days on the water when the strike of striped bass might be a fifty-pounder; to spring mornings when a cove on Roosevelt holds a dozen boats full of crappie fishermen, and they're all catching fish; to some high country lake to witness that magic moment when a smiling youngster holds up the first-ever trout; to lonesome streams where you can walk for three days without seeing another human footprint.

Welcome to hunting for bighorn sheep in the majestic desert ranges; to elk hunts in the Mogollon Rim's pine forests; to Mearns' quail on the glorious grassland and oak hillsides near Patagonia; to the inky blackness of a White Mountain pre-dawn, waiting for the big male turkey to gobble good morning and fly down from the roost tree.

Welcome to Outdoors in Arizona.

Two fishermen ready their rods and reels. It is always good to have a companion along to verify that story of "the one that got away." J. Peter Mortimer

Colorado River Country

"Too thick to drink and too thin to plow," they used to say about the Colorado as it raced through Arizona canyons. When the river was in flood stage, in late spring, it roared down from the north toward the Gulf of California, carrying a million tons of sediment past any given point every twenty-four hours.

That's all changed now; the muddy, brawling river has been tamed and dammed and managed. The big reservoirs — Powell, Mead, Mohave, and Havasu — are flung along the northern and western borders of our state like turquoise necklaces on a blanket of red, buff, and black. There are still rapids deep in the Grand Canyon, between Powell and Mead, but the water is cold now, and blue-green where it slices through the most ancient parts of the earth's crust.

The Colorado enters Arizona about halfway between Nevada and New Mexico as part of Lake Powell, the newest impoundment on the old river. Then it winds through Marble Canyon and on into the Grand Canyon, twisting and turning through the polished walls, buttes, and battlements for more than two hundred miles before it slows again for Lake Mead.

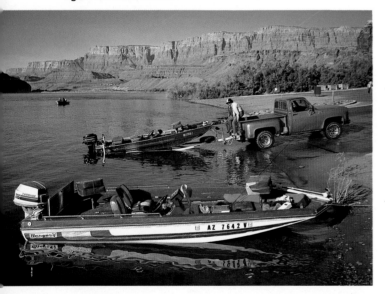

Below Hoover Dam, there is a short stretch of river, then the waters become placid once more as part of Lake Mohave. South of Davis Dam, the river flows through wild, lonesome country to Topock Gorge and Lake Havasu.

Ski boats and fishing craft now ply the waters once traveled by steamboats that worked their way up the Colorado to the mining towns and Army posts that, a century ago, were lone outposts in the wilderness.

Desert bighorn sheep, big mule deer, antelope, turkey, and small game roam the mountains along the Colorado and in the Strip, that forgotten chunk of Arizona that stretches north from the Grand Canyon to the Utah state line. Most of this area is lightly settled. Kingman and Page are two towns at opposite ends of the region, and there are thousands of square miles of solitude between them.

There's an old stone hotel perched on the edge of the North Rim of the Grand Canyon, like a castle with the world's greatest moat. To get to the castle, you must drive through the enchanted forest — the Kaibab National Forest. A similar forest guards the South Rim.

The North Kaibab is an ecological island, a long, forested plateau isolated by the Grand Canyon on the south and by desert lands on its other approaches. This is the home of a huge herd of mule deer. The record book is dotted with North Kaibab bucks, and their outsize antlers are popular with trophy hunters worldwide. If you drive State Route 67 between Jacob Lake and the North Rim early or late in the day, almost any day, you'll see deer, often dozens of them.

The forest holds turkey, blue grouse, and the unique Kaibab squirrel as well. And just off to the east is House Rock Valley, home of a herd of buffalo that are the descendants of animals brought to this area around the turn of the century. They were part of an experiment to cross buffalo and cattle to get a hardy meat producer that could thrive in the dry sagebrush flats.

God and man exhibit some of their best handiwork in this region. At each end of the Grand Canyon are soaring concrete dams, engineering marvels that have tamed the Colorado and provided smooth waterways where once the rapids raged. Lake Mead is the largest man-made lake in the country, Powell the second largest.

There is an aura of timelessness about Colorado River country: A day spent anywhere in this region is perfect medicine for an inflated ego. You can look endlessly at the Grand Canyon, or walk the Strip for eight hours without coming to a road. You can put your face against some ancient piece of granite that has been smoothed by the winds of centuries and discover that the world can get along without you after all. Here, as you take in the grandeur of hundred-mile vistas, you realize that you are just a tick in the eternity of time.

(Above left) You can launch a large bass boat easily at Lees Ferry, though smaller boats are more popular. Because of the swift current, an outboard of at least fifteen horsepower is a good idea. Tom Bean

(Right) The beaches below Glen Canyon Dam are popular stopping places, and fishing from the shore is excellent. The dam has changed the Colorado. It now slips through Marble Canyon as a cold, clear trout stream, far different from the muddy red torrent of old. James Tallon

(Left) The efforts of these happy anglers were rewarded with a ten-pound rainbow.

(Right) The daily bag limit of trout in the Lees Ferry area is four. But considering the size of the fish, this angler is still going to have plenty to eat.

(Below) Big rainbow trout—this one weighed more than six pounds—come from the section of the Colorado River below Glen Canyon Dam.

Photographs by James Tallon

(Left) Houseboats make perfect headquarters for fishing expeditions on lakes Powell, Mead, Mohave, and Havasu. This one is anchored in Oak Canyon on Powell, fifty miles uplake from the dam. Jerry Jacka

(Right) Some trout fishermen take their families along when they challenge the clear, cold waters of the Colorado River between Lake Powell and Lees Ferry. J. Peter Mortimer

(Below) Glen Canyon Dam backs up Lake Powell through more than 180 miles of dazzling red rock, creating more than ninety major side canyons and thousands of small, unnamed coves—a challenging paradise for anglers. James Tallon

(Below right) Largemouth bass are probably the most popular fish in Colorado River country, and every angler's ambition is to land one this big. It pulled the scale's needle down to the eight-pound mark. James Tallon

(Above) Lake Mead, the largest man-made lake in the United States, has some spectacular scenery. This rugged cliff is a wall of Iceberg Canyon.

(Right) Conditions at Mead and the other Colorado River lakes are far different from those of most of the U.S., and the clear water and unusual shoreline call for different techniques and different lures.

(Below) Temple Bar is the name of this imposing rock formation located just across Lake Mead from a marina of the same name. The marina is accessible by paved road north from U.S. Route 93.

Photographs by James Tallon

(Left) Sunrise on Lake Havasu, when the senses stir and both the day and the fisherman are full of hope.
Carlos Elmer

(Right) The waters of Lake Havasu have a reputation for catfish in the two-pound to four-pound size. Every now and then you hook into an Ol' Granddad like this one. Bob Hirsch

(Below) Willow Beach on upper Lake Mohave, where the rugged mountains watch over anglers seeking trout, stripers, bass, and catfish.
Tom Bean

(Far left) The Kaibab's mix of pine, spruce, and aspen, with many small meadows, is prime deer and turkey country. Dan Fischer

(Left) Wild turkeys are found throughout the Kaibab Plateau. James Tallon

(Below) The Kaibab forest is one of the premier places in the state to hunt mule deer. Hunters from all over the country come here looking for trophy bucks. Tony Mandile

(Following panel, pages 20-21) House Rock Valley, on the North Rim, is home to a fine herd of buffalo. The area is bounded by the Grand Canyon, the Kaibab Plateau, and, as shown in this painting, the Vermilion Cliffs. Larry Toschik

Region 1

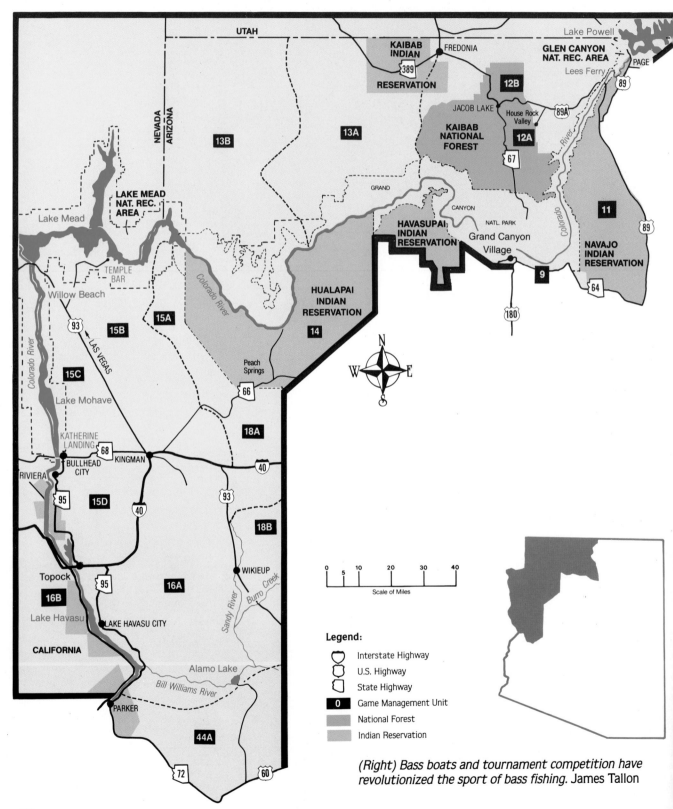

UTAH

KAIBAB INDIAN RESERVATION

FREDONIA

389

GLEN CANYON NAT. REC. AREA

Lake Powell

PAGE

Lees Ferry

12B

89

JACOB LAKE

House Rock Valley

89A

KAIBAB NATIONAL FOREST

12A

NEVADA

ARIZONA

13B

13A

67

11

Colorado River

LAKE MEAD NAT. REC. AREA

GRAND

CANYON

NATL. PARK

NAVAJO INDIAN RESERVATION

Lake Mead

HAVASUPAI INDIAN RESERVATION

Grand Canyon Village

89

TEMPLE BAR

HUALAPAI INDIAN RESERVATION

9

64

Willow Beach

15A

180

93

15B

LAS VEGAS

14

Peach Springs

66

N

W   E

S

15C

Lake Mohave

18A

KATHERINE LANDING

68

KINGMAN

BULLHEAD CITY

40

RIVIERA

95

15D

40

93

18B

WIKIEUP

Burro Creek

Topock

95

16A

Sandy River

0   5   10   20   30   40
Scale of Miles

16B

LAKE HAVASU CITY

Lake Havasu

CALIFORNIA

Alamo Lake

Legend:

⬡ Interstate Highway

⬡ U.S. Highway

⬡ State Highway

⬛0 Game Management Unit

▨ National Forest

▨ Indian Reservation

Bill Williams River

PARKER

44A

72

60

(Right) Bass boats and tournament competition have revolutionized the sport of bass fishing. James Tallon

Fishing the Colorado River Country

The Colorado River is a land of fishing superlatives. Everything is big here: The lakes are big; the river is big; the striped bass, trout, crappie, catfish, and largemouth bass are huge.

This happy state of affairs is due to the hand of man. When the first visitors from the Old World arrived, they found the Colorado running as red as its name, subject to massive flooding from snowmelt and spring rains and occasionally shrinking to a muddy trickle. The native fish were suckers and chubs that had adapted to the murky water and fierce flows.

Then, back in the 1930s, Boulder (Hoover) Dam was constructed, and the changing of the Colorado began. Lake Mead formed behind the dam and was stocked with largemouth bass, catfish, crappie, and bluegills. Parker Dam, impounding Lake Havasu, was followed by Davis Dam and Lake Mohave. And finally, in 1963, the gates closed on Glen Canyon Dam, and Lake Powell began to fill.

The Colorado is still a wild river in the depths of the Grand Canyon, but even there, the flow is controlled by releases from Lake Powell. And where the river once ran red and angry, it now flows with the blue-green hue that gave Havasu its name.

The four lakes thus formed were all stocked with largemouth bass, crappie, catfish, and panfish. Then two more stocks of fish further changed Colorado River fishing forever. The areas below each dam, the tailwaters, are cold, since the water is released from deep in the lake rather than from the warm surface. So for some miles below Glen Canyon, Hoover, and Davis dams, trout thrive, big trout made all the more remarkable because they come from desert surroundings.

In the early 1960s, the final item on the Colorado River fishing menu appeared—striped bass. They were introduced in Lake Havasu, and later planted in Mead and Powell. They have created a fishing sensation. Anglers accustomed to two- or three-pound largemouth bass fell in love with the ten- to twenty-pound stripers and when a forty- or fifty-pounder was taken, it became a thrill just to fish in a lake that contained a fish that big.

The Colorado River lakes are busy during the spring and summer months when water worshipers from all over the West enjoy the sunshine and wide-open watery spaces. But there are no seasons when the fish take a vacation, and if there is a single best bet for the Arizona angler, those lakes offer it.

Fishing

Lake Powell

Lake Powell's statistics are impressive. The lake is 186 miles long and has 1900 miles of shoreline. That's more than the distance between Mexico and Canada along the nation's West Coast. Add about one hundred major side canyons and thousands of small, unnamed coves, and you have enough cover to keep an angler busy forever.

Largemouth bass have been the mainstay at Powell since the lake began to fill, but now that the lake has matured, it's a bit tougher to take limits. As the lake filled, there was an explosion of the bass population. There was abundant food and cover, and predation was light. Now the bass are just one species among many.

April, May, and June are the top months; the fish are up in shallow water and easier to find. Powell's clear water means most bass are deep most of the time, but early and late hours are good for surface lures.

In murky water coves where some runoff has colored the water (or up the San Juan arm where the same thing occurs), medium running lures take fish consistently. Spoons, jigs, and plastic worms are a good bet anytime, and since they can cover water to depths of forty or fifty feet, they are necessary during months when the bass are deep.

Powell's crappie herds have become famous throughout the West. During the spring months, especially, the crappie schools move into shallow water coves. If the coves contain flooded brush or trees, so much the better. When spawning time comes, these great speckled beauties will even cozy up to a drowned tumbleweed.

Fish in the one- to two-pound class are common, and the daily limit of twenty crappies is not hard to achieve if you're in the right place at the right time. Small feather jigs in white or yellow work well; so do small, shiny lures that imitate the threadfin shad minnow, the crappie's favorite food. The March to May period is best, but there's often a fall "bite" as well. For the rest of the year, the crappies are deep and difficult to find.

Striped bass were stocked in Powell in the early 1970s. They have become one of the most popular species in the lake, partly because they are easiest to catch during the summer and fall months when most people are on the lake, and partly because they are plentiful. Like stripers in other Colorado River reservoirs, Powell's fish tend to get very large, and a striper from this lake is often the largest freshwater fish a visitor has ever taken. Stripers love shad, so shiny spoons and plugs work best. Trolling is a good bet to locate schools.

Walleye were never stocked in the lake, but the cold, clear water and the abundant rocky shoreline are just what walleye love best. So the few fish that apparently drifted down from upstream reservoirs have reproduced, and the population now exists throughout the lake. May is the best month for walleye, but they are taken year-round, often by anglers trying for bass or stripers. Most fishermen think the firm, white flesh of the walleye is the best eating of all fresh-water fish.

Powell's clear water means most of the catfish are caught at night, when they move up into shallower water to feed. Waterdogs, frozen anchovies, and night crawlers are most often used, and late spring, summer, and early fall are the best months. There are some huge bluegills in Powell along with the millions of the smaller variety. April and May are the months when bluegill spawn, and they move into quiet coves, especially where there is brush, in water two to eight feet deep. Worms, flies, and small maribou jigs work very well then, and this is the time the bigger fish are caught.

Six marinas serve Lake Powell, with a wide range of services for visitors, including hotels, rental boats, tours, and a large campground at Wahweap, near Page. The entire area is under National Park Service jurisdiction.

Powell is absolutely unique; there is no other lake like it anywhere. The surroundings are so awesome you really don't care whether you catch fish or not, but you almost always do!

Between Powell and Mead

Lees Ferry is a stretch of the Colorado River fourteen miles downriver from Glen Canyon Dam and Lake Powell that takes its name from a ferry boat crossing established more than a century ago. The ferry hasn't been in business since Navajo Bridge spanned the Colorado nearby in 1929. Anglers launch boats at Lees Ferry and run upstream toward the dam to fish for trout: rainbow, brook, and cutthroat.

The water temperature is about fifty degrees year-round, the water is clear, and there's abundant food, so the river here grows trophy fish. Two- to three-pound fish are common, five-pounders are taken daily, and trout over ten pounds are not all that unusual. In recognition of these unique circumstances, some special rules apply. These include reduced limits and methods of taking designed to keep the fourteen-mile stretch a true blue ribbon fishery.

Cliffs one thousand feet high guard the blue-green water, and the trout match the scenery. The October-through-February period is most popular, but good fish are caught year-round.

The river in the **Grand Canyon** also holds good trout, and some of the small feeder streams, such as Clear Creek, Bright Angel, Deer, and Tapeats creeks, hold fish. In fact, some of these small streams are spawning areas for huge trout during the winter and early spring months. If you hike into the canyon or take one of the float trips through it, take along a fishing outfit and some small, shiny spinning lures. You could pick up an extra memento of your trip.

The **Hualapai Indian Reservation** fronts on a big chunk

of the Colorado as it winds through the Grand Canyon, but access is only possible (by vehicle) at Diamond Creek, via the dirt road from Peach Springs. There is some trout fishing here, and the tribe does offer daily fishing permits.

Lake Mead

Lake Mead is the grizzled old veteran of the Colorado. Fishing for largemouth bass, crappie, and catfish suffered badly during the 1970s, while Lake Powell was filling, but the lake is back in business today as one of the best large-mouth bass and striped bass spots in the West.

The stripers are generally easier to catch and tend to run larger than the black bass, so they've been getting most of the attention recently. Look for surface action during the summer and fall as the striper schools herd concentrations of threadfin shad to the surface and attack them. These "boils" may last a few seconds to half an hour, though a minute or so is more like the average.

Las Vegas Wash, the area uplake from Temple Bar, Callville Bay, and Government Wash are striper hot spots. Look for stripers to be deep during the winter, shallower in the spring, often on top during the summer and early fall. Mead built its fishing reputation on largemouth bass, and that species is still a mainstay. The areas from Temple Bar uplake to Grand Wash are most popular, but there's no part of the huge lake that doesn't put out its share of bass.

During the spring, summer, and early fall months, action is divided among top water, deep-diving lures, and plastic worms and jigs. Jigs and spoons work best in the winter, when the bass tend to be in deeper, warmer water. The lake is so big and features so many miles of shoreline that it's possible to get back in some of the coves and fish for an entire day without seeing another angler.

Trolling is a popular way to take both largemouth and striped bass, and deep-diving plugs like the Hellbender and Rebel Deep Wee R catch a lot of Lake Mead bass. The water is often clear here, and light line — monofilament in the six- to eight-pound class — is a big help in fooling the bass. Long rods that enable anglers to make casts far in advance of the boat also help.

Shore access is so limited that it's nearly impossible to catch bass without a boat. Like the other Colorado River impoundments, Mead is big enough to get very rough when the wind blows, so those in smaller boats need to stay close to home and keep an eye on the weather.

Most Mead fishermen are after largemouth bass or strip-ers, but the lake also has excellent fishing for channel catfish and crappie. The cats prefer warm water, and they bite best from May to October. They're homely compared with the sleek bass, but they fight well and taste delicious on the table; so catfish have a large and dedicated fan club. Look for cats at night in water of twenty feet or less. Waterdogs, minnows (dead or alive), night crawlers, frozen anchovies, and all the various stink baits (including those homemade versions that are so vile they bring tears to the eyes) catch catfish. They occasionally hit artificial lures too.

Mead's crappie population is cyclic, as in most big reser-voirs. They begin to move into the shallows and show up on stringers in December or January, and the action lasts until late May or early June. The dingy waters of the Overton or Virgin River arms of the lake usually provide the first action, and as the season advances, other areas turn on. Live min-nows, small feather jigs, and tiny spoons and lures all account for their share of crappies. The big panfish are generally not aggressive, so they prefer a slow-moving lure.

There are the usual huge populations of small bluegills and green sunfish in Mead, and a hook baited with a worm will get instant action in any cove during the summer.

There are also big schools of carp in Mead, as there are in all the Colorado River lakes. American anglers tend to forget that carp were imported to this country more than a cen-tury ago because they were sporty and good to eat. That's still true, and carp from the clear waters of Mead do indeed fight well and taste fine when properly prepared. There's no limit on the number of carp you can catch. Try them on ultra-light spinning tackle or a flyrod for ultimate action.

Fillet the meat, cut it into bite-size pieces and score them deeply, then dip in egg, roll in cracker crumbs, and fry to a crisp brown. They really are delicious.

There are half a dozen full-service marinas on Mead, with everything from lodging to rental boats and guides, to campgrounds and stores, so the boater-angler can find any sort of service he needs.

Willow Beach

Willow Beach is the resort-marina-launch area eleven miles downriver from Hoover Dam. This section of Black Canyon is trout water, and the cold, clear currents coming from deep within Lake Mead are perfect for rainbow trout. A federal hatchery just upstream frcm the resort keeps the area well stocked.

Trout to three or four pounds are taken daily, and the cafe at the resort features pictures of happy fishermen with rainbows over five pounds. The Arizona record rainbow, a twenty-one-pound, five-ounce monster, came from here in September 1966.

Anglers boat upstream and fish deep backwater pools or drift-fish, bouncing worms or cheese bait along the bottom. Light line works best in the clear water. Shore anglers, fishing with bait in the area between the resort and the hatchery, do well on pan-size rainbows, with occasional big fish too. The trout bite all year, but the fall and early winter months are best for larger trout.

Fishing

Lake Mohave

Lake Mohave stretches sixty-seven miles from Hoover Dam downstream through rugged desert country to Davis Dam, dedicated in 1952. The long, narrow lake does not offer the large coves found on Mead and Powell, but it does have good sand beaches in many areas, and the long, sloping rock points offer good cover for fish.

Most access is from the two major resorts at Katherine Landing, just above the dam, and Cottonwood Cove, about midway along the western shore. Katherine is a full-service resort that also features a National Park Service campground. Because Mohave (like Lake Havasu, downstream) is comparatively close to California population centers, it gets more boating, skiing, and sightseeing traffic than Mead and Powell and a bit less from anglers. Fishermen tend to take over during the late fall and winter months.

Lake Mohave largemouth bass fishing is a bad news-good news situation. The bad news is that bass fishing generally is tougher here than at other Colorado River lakes. Most of the year, limits are hard to find. The good news is this lake puts out more big bass than the other reservoirs.

Bass come up into the shallows in late spring to spawn, and there's good top water and medium running lure action then. With some exceptions, the bass tend to stay deep the rest of the year. Anglers using waterdogs at depths of fifty or sixty feet catch bass; so do lure flingers who prospect at the same depths. Lots of bass above five pounds are taken at Mohave, and that tends to keep anglers coming back for another try.

Striped bass have drifted into Mohave from upstream Lake Mead, and they eventually will be widespread. A few years of successful spawning and growth, and the transplants should be showing from one end of the lake to the other. Although stripers relish threadfin shad, the ubiquitous forage fish, they also eat small rainbow trout. So the upper end of the lake, where trout are stocked, seems to be the place to find striped bass. As their population increases, it raises some questions about the future of trout stocks in the lake. Pan-size rainbows are very expensive fodder for stripers.

Rainbows are taken lakewide, but anglers tend to concentrate at Willow Beach at the north end of the lake, in the area near Cottonwood Cove and in the area from Katherine Landing to the dam. Most midlake fishing is from shore with bait. Worms, marshmallows, floating cheese bait, and salmon eggs are popular.

Trollers near the dam use lures like the Needlefish or Z-Rays at depths from fifty to one hundred feet or more, with leaded line the norm. Some anglers drift near the face of the dam and lower bait to whatever is the magic depth of that day. Trout to three to four pounds are taken all year, and spring fish tend to be shallower and easier to find.

Catfishing at Mohave is very good from late spring to early fall, and waterdogs and worms are used by most anglers. Sandy bottomed bays, fished at dusk and on into the night, are best.

On Down the River

The Colorado River between Davis Dam and the head of Lake Havasu can contain striped bass, largemouth bass, and trout; trout most often show during the winter months, the stripers and bass in late spring and summer.

Bullhead City, just below Davis Dam, is a hot spot for striped bass from April to September when the stripers run upriver from Havasu to spawn in the river below Davis. Since the water here is cold, it's a good place for trout as well, and both shore and boat anglers take fish to four or five pounds on bait and lures. Channel catfish also frequent this stretch, as do largemouth bass, which generally prefer the quiet, warmer backwater areas.

Big areas of flooded, brushy backwaters loop away from the river at **Topock,** and both bass and catfish are taken here during the warmer months. Crappies move into the shallows here as well, usually beginning in January and often continuing through April. Just downstream, between the Needles-Topock area and Lake Havasu, is **Topock Gorge.** The main river channel is lined with reeds that seem to present a solid wall, but there are narrow channels leading to hidden backwaters. These tend to warm up first in the springtime, so bass and catfish can often be caught before they begin to bite in the main river or the lakes.

Lake Havasu

Lake Havasu is formed by Parker Dam. At an elevation of 450 feet above sea level, it gets warm during the summer months. That warmth means big schools of striped bass on the surface (along with batches of bikini-clad girls on the beaches). If the striped bass are not up chasing shad, they are schooled in the deeper parts of the lake. They can be taken by boaters with drifting anchovies or big shiner minnows in depths to fifty feet or so.

Lake Havasu was the site of Arizona's first plant of striped bass, back in the early 1960s. The largest inland striper ever caught came from the river above Havasu in 1977. It weighed fifty-nine pounds, twelve ounces. Stripers in the twenty- to thirty-pound class are taken each year, and occasionally an angler tangles with a brute in the forty- or fifty-pound category.

Most anglers feel the present record (and the sixty-pound barrier) will be broken one day soon, probably with a fish from Havasu. The average fish is less than five pounds at Havasu, but there are lots of them and the possibility of a larger fish exists on every cast.

Largemouth bass were a Havasu favorite long before the

stripers were stocked, and they continue to offer sport. The lake offers quiet coves, big stands of reeds (tules, anglers call them), and abundant rocky shoreline, all good bass cover. Havasu's bass-holding tule beds popularized the sport of "flipping." This is the practice of using a long rod to drop small plastic worms or jigs into coffee-can-size holes in the reeds, then snatching out the bass that bites before it gets a chance to tangle the line. Most Havasu bass are in the one-to two-pound class and limits are not easy. To ensure larger bass for the future, there's now a 13" minimum size limit in effect and it seems to be working well.

Havasu's elevation and generally warm water give it a reputation as a top catfish lake. Channel cats in the two- to four-pound range decorate most stringers. They fall for waterdogs, minnows, worms, and a wide variety of stink baits. The lower half of the lake, especially around the Bill Williams arm, puts out most of the cats. Like most of their clan, they bite best when the water is warmest, and nighttime hours usually produce the top catches.

Some huge stringers of big crappie come from Havasu in those years when the population is up, and the Bill Williams arm of the lake, with its abundant tule beds, is usually the hot spot. Steamboat Cove is another crappie "hole," and when things are right, a string of two-pound fish is not unusual. Like the other Colorado River lakes, Havasu is full of carp, bluegills, and green sunfish. Children, whose minds are not yet cluttered with notions about which fish are best, enjoy catching them all.

There are eight resort-campground-marina complexes on the lake.

Alamo Lake

Alamo Lake is on the Bill Williams River, a tributary of the Colorado. Access is via a paved highway north of Wenden off U.S. Route 60. Alamo's surface acres fluctuate sharply, reflecting its primary role as a flood-control structure, but generally the lake contains two to three thousand surface acres. Alamo translates as "cottonwood" in Spanish, and many of the huge cottonwood trees that grew along the river have been inundated by the lake. They provide excellent bass cover.

The lake is basically sprawling, shallow, and usually murky, with many brushy coves and long, sloping points of rock and gravel. Alamo produces lots of largemouth bass, including trophy fish of five pounds and up every weekend. February through May is best, but the summer months are also excellent, especially early and late in the day and during nighttime hours when the bass are most active. Alamo is one of the best plastic-worm lakes in the state, and top water plugs that pop and gurgle are another good bet during the warmer months. It's tough to come away from Alamo without at least a few bass.

The lake is catfish paradise as well, and perhaps because the bass fishing is generally good, the cats are largely overlooked. The lake contains channel catfish, bullheads, and flathead cats, so the whiskered clan is well represented. Fish the mouths of the brushy coves late in the day and on into the night for best results. Cloudy, overcast days are good for cats at any hour. Waterdogs, worms, or shrimp work very well. Small "fiddler" channel cats are everywhere, so prevalent they are a nuisance, but a patient angler can expect fish in the two- to five-pound class and occasional flatheads over ten pounds.

Alamo's bluegill herds are not quite so plentiful as in the past, at least not the larger, hand-size fish. But late spring and early summer are still good times to use a flyrod and a small jig or wooly worm fly to load a stringer with husky, colorful bluegills.

There is an excellent Arizona State Park campground at the lake and a concession that offers rental boats and a well-equipped store.

Largemouth bass

Hunting the Colorado River Country

It seems fitting that some of the wildest, least-inhabited parts of Arizona would yield the biggest deer and be the home of the desert bighorn sheep, a true symbol of wilderness. This northwestern corner of our state offers hunting for all the game species on Arizona's hunt menu. They are found in country that makes hunting a real challenge: terrain that varies from thick timber to mini-Grand Canyons.

Deer Hunting

Although Arizona is far down the list of good deer states, we're well represented in the record book, and most of those trophy heads came from either the North Kaibab or the Arizona Strip.

Big mule deer are found throughout the state, but the country north of the Grand Canyon consistently produces the biggest and best of all. That portion of the state between the Grand Canyon and the Utah state line is commonly called the Strip, and Game Management Unit 13 represents this rugged piece of real estate. There are few roads and fewer people. There are some forested mountains, but most of the country is juniper and sage, and huge side canyons lead into the Grand Canyon. You might hunt this lower, desert-type country for a week and never glimpse a deer, then one day spot the largest one you've ever seen.

The North Kaibab is that high, forested plateau bisected by State Route 67 as it runs from Jacob Lake to the North Rim of the Canyon. This is the premier deer spot in the state. Success rates are generally high, and the chance to take a real trophy is better here than anywhere else in Arizona. Because this area (Unit 12A) offers such good hunting, the chance of getting drawn for one of the precious permits is low.

Units 15, 15A, 15B, 15C and 15D, north and west of Kingman, have one small rifle hunt but are otherwise set aside for muzzleloader and archery hunters only. Success rates are lower, but these hunters spend more time afield and gain great satisfaction from hunting with the so-called primitive weapons. This is rugged country with stands of thick juniper, just the kind of sneak and peek cover that archers and smokepole hunters relish.

Southeast of Kingman are the Hualapai Mountains in Unit 16A. Here the cover ranges from pines on the highest peaks to juniper on the lower ridges and paloverde-mesquite desert habitat in the lower reaches. This kind of mixed cover is always good deer country. Throw in the rugged nature of the range — you have to really want a deer to tackle some of it — and the result is an area with better than average figures for deer hunter success.

Elk Hunting

The Hualapai Indian Reservation — Unit 14 — curls around a big bend in the Colorado River's southern shore downstream from the most-viewed parts of the Grand Canyon. Elk were transplanted here in the 1960s, and the Hualapai now offer an early and late elk hunt, both with very limited permit numbers. Fees tend to be expensive — in the several-thousand-dollar range.

Hunter on the Kaibab Plateau. The plateau offers fir, spruce, pine, and aspen at 8000-foot elevations, then slopes to junipers and high desert. James Tallon

Antelope Hunting

Units 12A and 13A are not currently open to antelope hunting in this region, though that may change. Some of the largest antelope in the state have come from the Arizona Strip country in the past. Biologists will monitor the herds and decide when permits may be authorized, never more than the antelope numbers will justify.

The Hualapai tribe offers a few trophy antelope permits on their reservation each fall — usually in September. They are a good deal more expensive than state permits but they are sold on a first-come basis with no drawing.

Turkey Hunting

Units 12A and 13A offer spring and fall turkey hunts, and the Hualapai in Unit 14 also provide a limited number of spring and fall turkey permits. Fall hunters need not apply for a special permit. You simply buy a tag and take to the woods. Relatively few hunters — less than 100 — make the long trek to 13A's forested regions each fall, and success there is low. Spring hunters do much better. In fact, this is one of the best areas in the state as far as success on the spring gobbler hunt is concerned. Turkeys were transplanted to both 13A and 12A, and they have adapted and reproduced very well. Unit 12A, the North Kaibab, follows statewide success averages on the spring hunt but is significantly better in the fall.

Lion Hunting

This region does have a fairly constant lion population, but since much of the area is far from population centers, it gets little hunting pressure. The few animals taken do not represent a significant percentage of the statewide total.

Buffalo Hunting

The great, shaggy American bison — better known as the buffalo — is one of the symbols of the old, vanished, romantic West. The animals are not native to Arizona; our state was a bit too far south of the buffalo's range and lacked the vast short grass prairies. But a herd was imported to House Rock Valley back around the turn of the century, as part of an attempt by Col. "Buffalo" Jones to cross-breed them with cattle to produce an animal hardy enough to handle the rugged country and the cold winters. The experiment didn't work out, but the buffalo are still there and a limited hunt is held each year to keep the animal numbers in balance with available food supplies; permits are issued by a computer drawing. Once a hunter has taken a buffalo, he may not hunt again in Arizona; there is a one-buffalo-per-lifetime limit. House Rock Valley snugs up against the North Rim of the Grand Canyon on the south and the steep side of the Kaibab Plateau on the west, and the wild country suits the hunt perfectly. A big bull buffalo can weigh as much as 2000 pounds. Finding this wily creature in the juniper-oak canyons and thickly forested flats of House Rock would have challenged even the best of the old-time buffalo hunters.

Small-Game Hunting

There is some fair to good small game hunting in this region but because of its remote nature, not many people take advantage of it. If you've always wanted to bag a blue grouse, these big birds of the spruce-aspen forest are in at least fair supply in Unit 12A — the North Kaibab. It is a long journey but chances are better here than at most other Arizona high country grouse spots. Along the border between Units 12A and B and 13A, there are some chukar partridges, this being the only place where transplants have established huntable populations of the birds. Even so, most are taken incidentally by deer hunters.

The Kaibab squirrel is legal game in Units 12A and 13A. This species has only recently joined the game list, after being totally protected for many years. Weather and food supplies are the controlling factors on populations, rather

than hunting. Kaibabs have been transplanted to several forested mountain ranges in Units 13A and B and the squirrels have flourished in their new habitats. The Kaibab squirrels are found no place else in the world but in this area on the north rim of the Grand Canyon. The bulk of the population remains on the North Rim within Grand Canyon National Park, where no hunting is allowed.

Gambel's quail are hunted mostly in the Kingman area and south toward Wikieup and Alamo Lake, where populations range from good to excellent. **Cottontail rabbits** inhabit the same general areas. Both provide good hunting when population numbers are high.

The Colorado River from Lake Mead south to Havasu offers hunting for both **ducks** and **geese.** The Havasu National Wildlife Refuge, just upstream from Lake Havasu, winters good numbers of waterfowl, including large flocks of Canada geese. Alamo Lake is another good waterfowl spot, with ducks, Canada geese, and snow geese in residence during the December and January hunting season.

Kaibab squirrel

Region 2
The Navajo Reservation

Navajo names do not come easily from unpracticed tongues. If you haven't grown up with the language, it's difficult to say words like Lukachukai, Asaayi, Tsaile, or Todacheene. Even well-known Navajo areas like Canyon de Chelly are mispronounced. But coming from the lips of a Navajo, the names flow like liquid silver.

Casual visitors can delight in learning the proper inflection. These strange and musical names make their strange and wonderful places even more interesting to visit. They even seem to heighten the sense of discovery for the outdoor type.

The Navajo Indian Reservation still is largely unknown to most Arizona outdoorsmen. That means the lakes are uncrowded. The hunts are restricted by season and available habitat, and participation is limited enough to ensure they are real sport.

Outdoor recreation programs on the Navajo reservation were begun, and for many years administered, by various agencies of the federal government, most notably the U. S. Fish and Wildlife Service and the Bureau of Indian Affairs. More recently, the Navajo themselves have taken charge. Advice, and partial funding, may still come from the federal level, but the Navajo are increasingly paying for the development of their recreational programs. Young people are leaving the reservation, getting degrees in wildlife management, and returning to join the staff of the Navajo Fish and Wildlife Agency.

There is genuine enthusiasm among biologists and administrators. For example, until 1984, all the trout stocked on the reservation came from federal hatcheries, mostly those on the Fort Apache reservation. The Navajo reservation has some lakes, mostly man-made, but no streams of the type usually considered adequate as a source of water for a trout hatchery.

But the thrust of the Navajo Fish and Wildlife Agency is toward self-determination. So biologists found a small stream with a flow of just ten gallons per minute — about twice what your garden hose puts out — and decided they could use this trickle as a water source for the first hatchery ever built on an Indian reservation without federal funds.

Local labor pitched in to build a pipeline from the spring to a small hatchery building. The finished product was not fancy, but the pipeline fed into a stack of hatching trays, raceways, and finally a small holding pond. The fish were hatched, raised to a certain size indoors, moved to outdoor raceways for more growth, then to the pond to put on a final spurt before being stocked in one of the reservation lakes. Ten thousand rainbows were raised the first year. Total cost of the hatchery: $18,000.

Most of the Navajo hunting, fishing, and camping takes place in the Chuska Mountains, along the border of Arizona and New Mexico. Even those who think they really know the Navajo reservation are often surprised to find this big range of pine-covered peaks, complete with aspen-ringed meadows and startling, tiny blue lakes. It's far different from Monument Valley.

Thus the special feeling of discovery the first time you follow the highway into the Navajo high country. You know others have been here before you, but for a day or two this little corner of paradise seems to have been created just for you.

(Right) Archery hunters get a chance to hunt turkey along with deer on a combination hunt early in the fall. Judd Cooney

(Far right) Most hunting on the Navajo Indian Reservation is confined to the Chuska Mountains, near the Arizona-New Mexico border. It's rugged, lonesome country. Jerry Jacka

(Above) Increasingly, Navajo officials administer hunting and fishing activities on the reservation. At the tribe's trout hatchery, built without federal funds, workers deploy a large net to collect fish for distribution to reservation lakes. James Tallon

(Left) Wheatfields Lake, north of the Navajo capital of Window Rock, is one of the most popular trout lakes on the reservation. Jerry Jacka

(Top) Mourning dove. Inge Martin

(Above) A rugged canyon in Navajo country. Jerry Jacka

(Right) The northern end of the Chuska Mountains, near Lukachukai—not countryside typical of the Navajo reservation, but good game habitat. David Muench

(Following panel, pages 36-37) From the deserts to the mountains, mule deer share the wild country of most of Arizona. Larry Toschik

Region 2

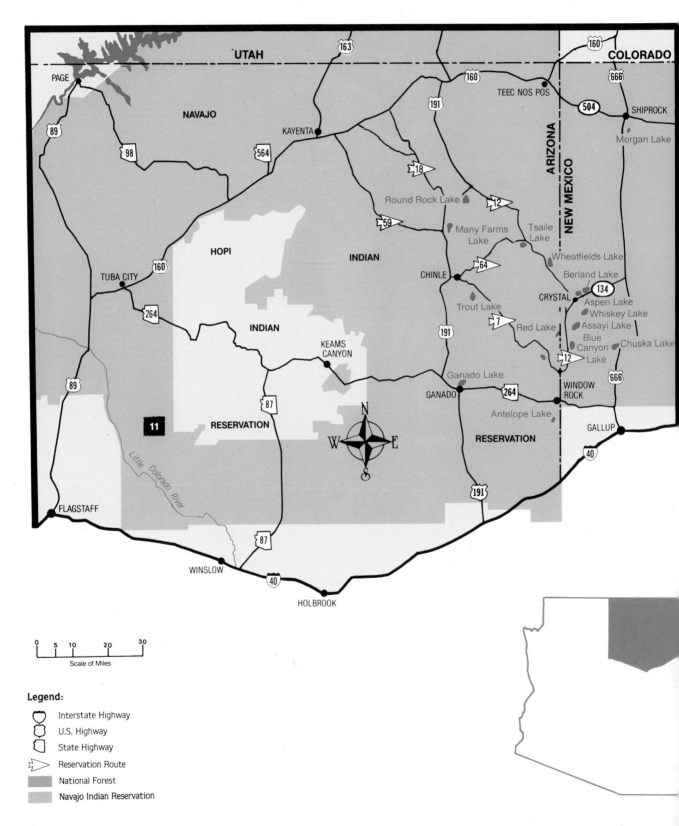

Legend:

- Interstate Highway
- U.S. Highway
- State Highway
- Reservation Route
- National Forest
- Navajo Indian Reservation

Scale of Miles
0 5 10 20 30

Fishing the Navajo Reservation

Most visitors are surprised to learn the Navajo Indian Reservation has trout lakes. Cold, clear trout lakes in high, pine meadows don't jibe with the popular notion that Navajoland is all red rock and sagebrush, juniper ridges, and flocks of sheep. The majority of the 16 million acres on the reservation are more like the popular conception, but along the Arizona-New Mexico border, from Window Rock to Lukachukai, stretch the Chuska Mountains. They contain pine, spruce, fir, and aspen, plus a dozen lakes stocked with trout. Elsewhere on the reservation are warm water lakes with bass and catfish.

There were squawfish and suckers in the San Juan River and perhaps small minnows in some of the tiny streams in the Four Corners area, but historically the Navajo did not fish, either for fun or food. Only in the last generation or so have they begun to turn to angling.

Non-Navajo fishing pressure is light, with most coming from the Gallup, New Mexico, area and from the reservation itself. Not many fishermen from the population centers of Phoenix and Tucson make the long trip, concentrating instead on the more accessible fishing in the White Mountains and along the Mogollon Rim. But lack of pressure and generally good fishing make the Navajo lakes worth considering. The pace is unhurried, the landscape is spectacular, and there's a good chance your stringer will be decorated with some fish of impressive size.

Included in this coverage of Navajo fishing waters are a number of lakes in New Mexico. The Chuska Mountains straddle the Arizona-New Mexico border, and Navajo Route 12, the primary road to many of the trout lakes, also wanders back and forth from state to state. Because no state license is needed to fish Navajo waters, we have listed lakes in both states. Simply buy a Navajo fishing permit and fish where you like.

Most Navajo fishing regulations parallel those of the Arizona Game and Fish Department, but there are some important exceptions, so be sure to pick up a copy of the Navajo rules when you buy your special fishing permit. The main difference is in bag limits. The Navajo allow fewer fish per day of trout, bass, and catfish. For anglers under 12, no license is needed, but daily limits are half those of adults or licensed anglers.

The Navajo fishing season is open year-round, but trout waters are open only from one-half hour before sunrise to one-half hour after sunset. A special boating permit is required to operate a boat on Navajo waters.

Wheatfields Lake

Wheatfields Lake is perhaps the best known of the trout waters. At 270 surface acres, it is larger than the other trout lakes on the reservation and access is no problem — paved Navajo Route 12 runs right across the dam. There's a casual campground in the pines near the dam; a small store sells fishing and picnic supplies. Boaters will find a launch ramp; electric motors only are allowed. Rainbow trout are the primary target, but the lake also contains brook and cutthroat trout.

Fishing is best in the spring and fall, and weeds are a problem in the warm summer months. The lake usually freezes in winter, and because access is easy, it's one of the most popular ice-fishing lakes in the January-to-March period, with some nice fish being taken then.

Tsaile Lake

Tsaile Lake (say'lee) developed some leakage problems on the spillway in the early 1980s, but after a two-year hiatus is now back in the business of producing good trout. It's a mile off Navajo Route 12, just a few miles north of Wheatfields, and at 260 surface acres is about the same size as that lake. Rainbow trout are most often caught, but Tsaile has some cutthroats, too, and is well stocked with channel catfish. This trout-catfish combination seems to work out well; the two species are apparently compatible.

Access is a problem on the eastern, or Route 12, side of the lake. There is a drive around to the western side to park and launch a boat, and electric motors only are allowed. Spring and fall months are best for trout, and Tsaile has a reputation for growing some large fish. Navajo Community College is at the northern end of the lake. You drive through the campus on your way to the dam-park-launch area. Some days it seems the trout have gone to college, too, so easily do they outwit the anglers.

Antelope Lake

Antelope Lake is just three acres, lightly fished, stocked with rainbows, and is in the southern end of the Chuska range, a few miles south of State Route 264, with the turnoff west of Window Rock. Antelope is weedy in summer, so spring and fall are best. Look for some lunker trout in the springtime, just after the ice melts. Electric motors only are allowed if you use a boat. There are no facilities and not much competition.

Trout Lake

Trout Lake is twenty-six surface acres, is stocked with rainbow trout each spring, and gets light pressure from anglers. It's in open, sagebrush country, south of Navajo Route 7 — the road to Sawmill — in the country north and west of Fort Defiance. There are no facilities, and electric motors only are permitted.

Chuska Lake

Chuska Lake is 25 miles north of Gallup, just off U.S.

Fishing

Route 666. It is stocked with rainbows, and fish in the seventeen- to eighteen-inch range are possible. There are no trees here and no facilities. The surface acreage is twenty-five, and electric motors only is the rule. Most fishing pressure comes from Gallup anglers.

Blue Canyon Lake

Blue Canyon Lake, normally the deepest lake on the reservation, at seventy-five feet, now contains walleye. Check with the tribal game and fish office for current details. The lake is just off Navajo Route 12, north of Fort Defiance.

Round Rock Lake

Round Rock Lake is another fishing hole that features a combination of rainbow trout and channel catfish. It is set in the red rock country on Navajo Route 12, north of Wheatfields and Tsaile and just south of the small community of Round Rock. The lake has fifty surface acres, allows electric motors only, and there are no facilities. Round Rock looks more like a catfish pond than a trout water, but it has the reputation for putting out big rainbows.

Assayi Lake

Assayi Lake is eleven miles east of Navajo, New Mexico, via an unpaved road, but access during the snow-free months is no problem for any sort of vehicle. There are thirty-six acres of trout lake here, electric motors only, and nothing much in the way of facilities. Rainbows and cutthroats are stocked. Fishing is best in April, May, and June and again in October and November. Ice fishing is available in years when a good freeze makes it safe.

Aspen Lake (Pond)

Aspen Lake, just an acre, is stocked with rainbow trout is north of New Mexico Route 134 and the community of Crystal, New Mexico. It is limited to electric motors, and there are no facilities.

Berland Lake

Berland Lake is just north of Aspen on the same unpaved but good access road. The local anglers go here to get away from the crowds, a relative term, on Wheatfields Lake. Berland has just three acres of water, is limited to electric motors, and has a few tables sprinkled among the pines. Rainbow trout thrive in the lake.

Long Lake

This shallow trout producer is about one and one-half miles NW of Whiskey Lake. It has rainbows, including some outsized ones. The tribe is considering restrictive regulations here—check before you fish.

Toadlena Lake

A small (35 acres) trout lake about 5 miles north of Berland Lake. It is stocked with rainbow trout, no monsters, just fat, scrappy fish that are mostly pan-sized. No facilities, electric motors only.

Whiskey Lake

Whiskey Lake is known for puns (take a drink of Whiskey!) and super trout growth. Rainbows stocked here gain up to two inches per month, at least twice the rate claimed by other "good" lakes. Whiskey is 250 acres, but it tends to be shallow and there's always a chance of winter freeze-ups and trout die-off. The Navajos are looking at Whiskey as a quality fishing lake, perhaps restricted to lures and flies only and/or with a reduced limit or a minimum size for keeper fish. The lake is in the pine-aspen country, just north of Assayi Lake on Navajo Route 30.

Ganado Lake

Ganado Lake is a 300-acre lake that supports mostly channel catfish, with an occasional largemouth bass. Its shallow, warm waters do grow good cats. Electric motors only is the rule here, and the spring and summer months offer the best fishing. The lake is about three miles north of the town of Ganado on Navajo Route 27.

Many Farms Lake

Many Farms Lake is 1000 acres and contains largemouth bass and catfish, with a chance at big bass. Many Farms is one of two lakes on the reservation where no motor restrictions are in effect. The lake is just outside the community of Many Farms, north of Chinle on U. S. Route 191.

Red Lake

Red Lake is to the west of Navajo Route 12, just north of the town of Navajo. The broad (600 acres), shallow lake is usually muddy, and it's easy to see how it got its name. Channel catfish are the main item on the fishing menu here, with an occasional largemouth bass. There are also rumors of northern pike. They were stocked many years ago, and there's a chance some may have survived, although fishery biologists for the tribe have been unable to verify their presence. Electric motors only are allowed on Red Lake.

Morgan Lake

Morgan Lake is south and east of Shiprock, New Mexico. It is the water-cooling reservoir for the Four Corners power plant, and since the water is always warm, there's no winter freeze and the fish grow year-round. Morgan contains largemouth bass, channel catfish, and bluegill. Though the average bass is much smaller, largemouths to eleven pounds have been reported. The lake is popular with anglers from Farmington, New Mexico, a few miles east. There's a boat-launch area, and the lake has no motor restrictions on its 1200 acres.

Hunting the Navajo Reservation

Although the Navajo reservation covers a large section of northeastern Arizona, hunting opportunities are slim. Most of the big and small-game hunting is concentrated in the Chuska Mountains, along the border of Arizona and New Mexico. A Navajo hunting permit allows hunting in either state without an additional license. Big-game hunting is by permit only, and Navajo and non-Navajo compete by drawing for the available mule deer or turkey tags. The Navajo reservation has a good population of bear, but they are not hunted. Success rates on both big and small game are generally low.

Deer Hunting

Mule deer hunters have a choice of two hunts. They may elect to hunt with a bow during the early October combination season for deer and turkey, or they can participate in the rifle hunt in November.

The archery season is restricted to a certain number of permits, but permitees may hunt in any of the five Navajo hunt units and any deer is legal. Although the archery deer-turkey permits are not expensive, they do not generally sell out. Success on the archery deer hunt varies from unit to unit, but is generally higher than the statewide figures.

Best areas are Tribal Game Units 1 and 2, on the northern end of the Chuska Mountains, and most deer are taken during the later part of the season. The units are large, and hunting pressure is light, so the Navajo hunt would seem to be a good bet for archers.

The November rifle hunt is by permit, chosen by a drawing. Both Navajo and non-Navajo compete for the same permits, but non-Navajo hunters are restricted to five percent of the total, and permits are good only for the specific unit for which they are issued. The southern parts of the Chuskas, Tribal Game Units 4 and 5, offer about the same chances of success to rifle hunters as the popular northern areas. Overall success for the rifle hunts is about the same as the statewide averages for Arizona — twenty to twenty-five percent.

Some trophy mule deer are taken each year on the reservation, and while it's difficult to get drawn, the chance to hunt the high juniper-pine country for a few days without seeing another hunter makes it all worthwhile. In too many of our state's hunt units, there are enough people afield to move the deer around during the day, and often you're shooting at animals that have been spooked by someone else. Most of the time on the Navajo reservation you are one on one with the muleys on their home territory, and if you bring home a good buck you've earned it.

Turkey Hunting

You can hunt turkey on the archers' combination deer-turkey hunt in early October, participate in the late November firearms season, or choose the spring gobbler hunt. All are permit hunts, but the permitee may choose any of the five Navajo units. Success rates are generally good on the firearms hunts, but only a few hunters take advantage of the seasons.

Small-Game Hunting

There is some **dove** hunting on the reservation, and the small-game license does cover animals such as prairie dogs. But generally the only opportunities available under this permit are waterfowl, including **ducks** and **geese** on the lakes and cattle-watering ponds.

Merriam's turkeys

Region 3

North Central Arizona

It's a long way from Happy Jack to Bumblebee, and even farther from the pine-clad slopes of Kendrick Mountain to the shoulders of Mount Mahon, across the Aquarius range from Wikieup. An outdoors fan could spend a lifetime exploring here and never kick out every covey of quail from every draw, or fail to be amazed as five big mule deer explode out of a piece of cover not thick enough to hide a rabbit.

If some genie should grant you three wishes, make one of them enough time to camp beside every pine, every oak, and every juniper in this huge expanse of Arizona landscape.

Some back-country enthusiasts rate roads by how long you have to wait before somebody comes along to help in case your vehicle breaks down. "Never" is perfect for some. They want a road whose exact location is zealously guarded, a place where they can count on not being disturbed by anybody, anytime. (Strange how a person who knows about a "good" road like this can look you right in the eye, smile, and give you explicit directions to a spot 200 miles away.) There are many "good" roads in this region, offering visitors the chance to get away — really away.

You may find an angler at Bull Pen Ranch on West Clear Creek who, after three days of fishing his way through the deep chasm that holds the stream, has a certain look in his eye. It's a reflection of wildness and peace.

You may meet a fisherman on Oak Creek who has just traversed the narrow canyon of the West Fork and suddenly seems to have emerged into the real world. If you ask him to show you the trout he caught, he'll smile and say, "I roasted two for dinner, wrapped 'em in foil, threw 'em in the campfire coals, and then ate them with my fingers right from the package. Best meal I've ever had. I threw back the rest of the rainbows to pay my check." That's pretty low-cost rent for an outdoor mansion like West Fork canyon.

In autumn, the hatchery trucks have ceased their visits to the area's streams, but the leftover trout are larger and smarter than their summer cousins and thus provide a stronger challenge. The season for bandtail pigeon, squirrel, and turkey opens in October, and waterfowl become part of a hunter's schedule about the same time.

This is big-game country, too — as big as a huge bull elk, or a buffalo, or a mule deer slipping away through the chaparral and leaving you only a glimpse. And there is other game as petite as a whitetail deer or an antelope, bathed in the early morning light and parading through silvery meadow grasses.

This region offers such a variety of things to do that it's easy to call it the heart of Arizona. It's not placed exactly right, geographically, to be the heart, but those who spend their outdoor time here will overlook that. The unique blend of mountains, rolling grasslands, rugged breaks of chaparral, and high desert presents a healthy sample of everything Arizona contains.

(Above) A few gray squirrels share the ponderosa forest with their more abundant cousins, the Abert squirrels. Inge Martin

(Left) Lynx Lake is popular, in part, because of easy accessibility from Phoenix and Prescott. Dick Dietrich

(Right) Quail hunting is best in the lower elevations along the west side of the region. James Tallon

(Left) Oak Creek continues to delight trout fishermen, as it has for decades. The accessible stretches are stocked weekly during the May-September season. Catching a rainbow takes on added pleasure when it happens amidst such scenic splendor. Dick Canby

(Below) Thousands of youngsters have taken their first trout from the friendly waters of Oak Creek—an ideal destination for families. Carlos Elmer

(Following panel, pages 46-47) White Horse Lake is typical of the small trout lakes tucked away in the pine country of this region. Anglers here can cool off and catch trout too. Dick Dietrich

(Top) A dad's advice is valuable—offered here at Lake Mary. Tom Bean

(Center) Northern pike waters in this region include Lake Mary, Mormon Lake, Stoneman Lake, and Long Lake. James Tallon

(Left) Fishing at Lake Mary. The long, narrow lake contains northern pike, walleye, and catfish. Tom Bean

(Top) There are not as many javelina in north central Arizona as in the southern part of the state, but hunter success is high. Robert Campbell

(Center) Abundant Gambel's quail make for excellent hunting in the high desert areas in the western part of this region. Robert Campbell

(Left) The rugged Sycamore Canyon Wilderness Area holds deer, bear, and lion. If you want to get away from the crowd, this is the place. Dick Dietrich

(Following panel, pages 52-53) Swift and beautiful antelope are found on the wide open rangelands of central Arizona. Larry Toschik

Region 3

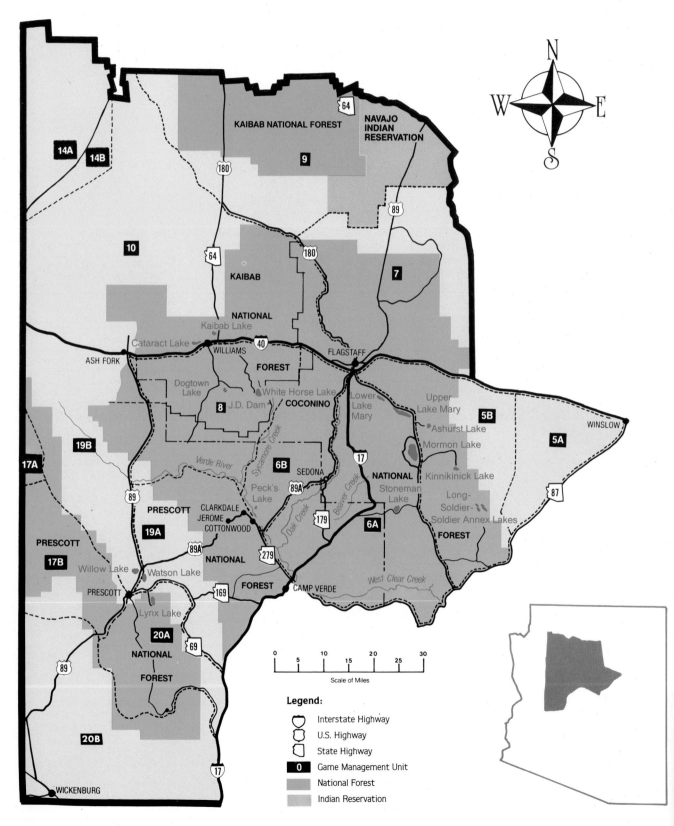

KAIBAB NATIONAL FOREST

NAVAJO INDIAN RESERVATION

64

9

14A   14B

180

10

64

180

89

KAIBAB

7

NATIONAL

Kaibab Lake

Cataract Lake

ASH FORK

WILLIAMS

40

FLAGSTAFF

FOREST

Dogtown Lake

White Horse Lake

8   J.D. Dam

COCONINO

Lower Lake Mary

Upper Lake Mary

5B

5A

WINSLOW

Ashurst Lake

19B

Verde River

Mormon Lake

17A

6B   SEDONA

17

NATIONAL

Kinnikinick Lake

89

Sycamore Creek

Peck's Lake

89A

Stoneman Lake

Long-Soldier-

PRESCOTT

CLARKDALE

Soldier Annex Lakes

JEROME

19A

179

6A

COTTONWOOD

FOREST

PRESCOTT

89A

Oak Creek

Beaver Creek

17B

NATIONAL

279

Willow Lake

Watson Lake

FOREST   CAMP VERDE

West Clear Creek

PRESCOTT

169

Lynx Lake

20A   69

NATIONAL

FOREST

89

20B

17

WICKENBURG

0   5   10   15   20   25   30

Scale of Miles

Legend:

Interstate Highway

U.S. Highway

State Highway

0   Game Management Unit

National Forest

Indian Reservation

Fishing North Central Arizona

Diversity is the name of the fishing game in Arizona, both in types of water and kinds of fish.

You can hike up the rugged canyon of West Clear Creek and play mind games with the broad-shouldered brown trout in some of the deep pools. Those feisty fish live between walls that stretch up a thousand feet on each side, and the water is ice cold. You either swim or back off.

Or, perhaps, you can spend a day at Lynx or Ashurst Lake and fish from the shore with your family. You might even doze a bit in your lawn chair while you wait for the trout to bite. In the heart of Arizona there is everything from rainbow trout to channel catfish, and only those who catch them can tell which is the most beautiful.

Stoneman Lake

Stoneman Lake is the only permanent lake in Arizona that isn't man-made. It's nestled in an old volcanic crater and exists without any dam. Northern pike and yellow perch are found here. The perch are often a pound or better, and most of the pike are a couple of pounds. There is a ring of reeds, forty or fifty feet from shore, making it difficult to fish without a boat. Motors are restricted to electrics. The lake is seventy acres, so cartoppers, canoes, or inflatables work fine. No live minnows are allowed, so use spoons or plugs for pike and worms or small feather jigs for perch. Shoreline access by vehicle is limited to a parking lot and boat launch ramp at the western end of the lake. Take the road heading east from the Stoneman Lake interchange on Interstate 17 south of Flagstaff. There are no developed campgrounds.

Mormon Lake

Mormon Lake is shallow, weedy, and hard to fish. It occasionally dries up. But there are plentiful bullheads and good numbers of northern pike, including some big ones. The lake is up to 600 acres when full and is about twenty-five miles southeast of Flagstaff on the Lake Mary-Mormon Lake Road. National forest campgrounds on the west side.

Upper and Lower Lake Mary

Upper Lake Mary has northern pike, walleye, and catfish. It is a long, narrow lake that winds along the paved highway about fifteen miles south of Flagstaff. There's a boat launch near the dam, and no motor restrictions are in effect. Pike like anything shiny, and casting or trolling spoons or wobbling plugs work well. Many anglers use waterdogs or cut bait like smelt or anchovy and take a shot at catching all three species of fish. The lake fills to 600 acres. Lakeview and Pine Grove campgrounds are nearby.

Lower Lake Mary is smaller (100 acres), shallower, and much more likely to be low and unfishable. You'll find the same species as at the upper lake, but this one is a mile or two closer to Flagstaff.

Kinnikinick Lake

Kinnikinick has 120 acres and is nine miles from the Lake Mary-Mormon Lake Road via Forest Roads 124 and 82 which are often rough. There are some big brown trout, but the lake mostly has catchable-size rainbows. Fall fly fishing is effective, and trolling is a good way to take trout anytime. There is a small campground.

Northern pike

Fishing

Ashurst Lake

Ashurst Lake is the area's most popular lake. The 200-acre lake is about twenty miles south of Flagstaff by the paved Lake Mary-Mormon Lake Road and Forest Road 82E. There are mostly pan-size rainbow trout, with an occasional brook trout. Sometimes the lake freezes hard enough that ice fishing is safe, usually in January-February.

Ashurst is popular with families who usually fish from shore and use salmon eggs or worms. The lake tends to get warm during the summer months, a time when trolling deep will find the trout. There's a campground with boat launch and parking lot; outboard motors to eight horsepower are permitted.

Three Lakes

Long, Soldier, and Soldier Annex Lakes are all connected, so fish stocked in one eventually end up in all three. They contain northern pike, walleye, largemouth bass, catfish, and bluegill, including very large specimens of each species. The lakes are generally quite muddy, making fishing tough. Long, at seventy acres, is the largest, and there are no motor restrictions. Soldier and Soldier Annex are small and come under the electric-motor-only rule. The best access is via Forest Roads 211 and 82 from the Blue Ridge Ranger Station beside State Route 87, north of Clint's Well.

Kaibab Lake

Kaibab Lake is two miles east of Williams, then one mile north on State Route 64—the Grand Canyon Highway. Kaibab's sixty-five acres hold rainbow and brown trout, mostly pan-size. Outboard motors to eight horsepower are allowed here, but most anglers fish from shore. Like all lakes in the Williams area, Kaibab is loaded with green sunfish and golden shiners. Both species compete fiercely with trout for space and food. So the lake gets plants of catchable-size trout on a regular basis. There's a nice Kaibab National Forest campground here.

Cataract Lake

Cataract Lake has just forty-five acres and is on the western edge of Williams. Although eight-horsepower engines are allowed here, most anglers fish from shore. Rainbow and brown trout, with some big browns taken in early spring. Otherwise, the lake is full of "trash" fish, which limits its productiveness. There is a small campground.

White Horse Lake

White Horse Lake is a popular trout lake and contains some good channel catfish. Rainbow trout are the main species, with an occasional brown also being taken. The lake is forty acres and features a store and boat rental. Boating is restricted to electric motors. White Horse is twenty miles south and east of Williams via Forest Roads 109 and 110, both passable by any sort of vehicle. A big national forest campground is located on the lakeshore.

J.D. Dam

J. D. Dam is small and usually murky. It is stocked with brown trout and restricted to the use of artificial lures and flies only; no bait is allowed. Browns are harder to fool than other kinds of trout, and the no-bait rule makes it even tougher. Ten-acre J. D. is best in spring or fall when the water is coldest. It is about five miles south of Whitehorse Lake on Forest Road 110, which is likely to be rough.

Dogtown Lake

Dogtown Lake, at fifty acres, is the largest in the area. It's six miles southeast of Williams via Forest Road 140. Boats are restricted to electric motors. The lake contains rainbows and browns, plus illegally stocked crappies that are generally too small to keep. It has tiny green sunfish too. Bait from shore works O.K. for the trout. There is a Kaibab National Forest campground.

Peck's Lake

Horseshoe-shaped Peck's Lake is seventy-seven acres on the edge of Clarkdale in the Verde Valley. Peck's has no motor restrictions, and occasionally somebody tries water skiing on the small body of water. There is a little of everything in the way of fish: carp, northern pike, largemouth bass, green sunfish, redear sunfish, and crappie. The lake gets lots of day use from Verde Valley residents. Peck's is another lake that has benefitted greatly by having its weeds harvested by the Arizona Game and Fish Department weed cutter.

Lynx Lake

Lynx Lake is a pretty little lake on one of the most famous gold-bearing creeks in Arizona. The gold here now, however, is rainbow trout, stocked every few weeks during the summer, and monthly during the winter. The lake covers about fifty acres, is restricted to electric motors, and is most often fished from shore. You'll find a store and boat-rental dock, a parking lot, and a free boat launch provided by Prescott National Forest, which also provides the campground. Lynx is seven miles southeast of Prescott via State Route 69 and Forest Road 197. Readily accessible to the million-plus people in the Phoenix area, Lynx gets heavy fishing pressure during the May-September period.

Watson, Willow Lakes

Watson and Willow lakes are a pair of small lakes, fifty and twenty acres respectively, on opposite sides of U. S. Route 89 about three miles north of Prescott. Both are irrigation-storage reservoirs, and their levels are subject to sharp drawdowns. When they have adequate supplies of water, both grow bass, catfish, crappies, and miscellaneous sunfish. Neither has motor restrictions. Access to Willow is closed.

Stream Fishing

Beaver Creek is small, like many other Arizona trout streams. Most of the fishing is in the short stretch of creek near the U. S. Forest Service campground and ranger station. Catchable rainbow trout, eight to nine inches, are stocked here in late spring and early summer, but the water gets too warm for continued stocking by late June or early July. There may be a few larger fish upstream — for hikers only — but this is the classic "put and take" stream. The hatchery truck puts the fish in and fishermen take them back out, so few remain at the end of the summer. Access is three miles east of the Sedona-Rimrock interchange on Interstate Route 17.

West Clear Creek has more than twenty-five miles of stream in a deep canyon amid some of the most rugged country in the state. A few four-wheel-drive-only roads poke tentatively toward the rim of the canyon, where a steep hiking trail or two wind into the depths. The creek heads up in the pines west of Clint's Well and joins the Verde River about seven miles east of Camp Verde. There are rainbow and brown trout in the deep pools, but only for the hardy and adventuresome. Some catchable rainbows are stocked at Bullpen Ranch, a few miles above the Verde, early in the summer as water temperatures permit.

Oak Creek: Most fishing takes place in the fifteen miles or so between Sedona and the head of the canyon. There are some places where the creek loops away from the road. But for most of its length the water is just a few steps from the pavement. Most of the catchable rainbows, stocked weekly during the summer months, are caught within a few days. Private holdings along the creek limit access and put added pressure on those stretches that can be fished. This is definitely not the place for lovers of solitude, but scenic beauty abounds and catching enough rainbows for lunch is usually not difficult. Lots of resorts and Coconino National Forest campgrounds.

Verde River begins in Chino Valley near the railroad siding of Paulden, winds through lonesome country past Perkinsville, Sycamore Canyon, and the towns of Cottonwood and Camp Verde, then turns southward toward Phoenix. There are lots of catfish in the river, especially in the stretch near Cottonwood, and some big ones in more remote sections. Night crawlers or shrimp, or a combination of the two, drifted slowly through deep pools will catch cats. Leave civilization behind for the best catches.

Rainbow trout

Hunting North Central Arizona

Some of the state's most popular hunting areas are in the Flagstaff-Williams-Prescott region. If you were forced to hunt only in the game-management units that make up this area, you would still be able to pursue all the major big and small game animals that Arizona has to offer.

And you would do it in a wide range of habitat types and elevations, from a few hundred feet above sea level near the western border of the state to 11,000-plus feet high on the San Francisco Peaks near Flagstaff.

The big-game hunting here, as elsewhere in the state, is by permit only. Look over the hunt menu that the Arizona Game and Fish Department makes up each spring, make your selection, fill out an application, then wait impatiently while the computer decides your fate.

You can opt for togetherness and join the big crowds that hunt in the pines south of Flagstaff, or you can walk a desert wash north of Date Creek and count on seeing few others of your kind for days at a time.

Deer Hunting

Most of the deer hunting units in this region are close to the statewide average for success. Most of the bucks are **mule deer,** but a few **whitetails** are taken in Units 5, 6, and 8, and there is a late hunt (December) in Units 6 and 8 for whitetails only. The success ratio here is a good deal better than the average.

The best place to hunt deer is an area you have hunted before, a place where you are familiar with the terrain and the deer's food, water, and rest areas—and their escape routes. All of the units in this region have decent populations of deer.

Unit 5 is generally pine country, with some antelope grassland in the northern sections. Parklike stands of ponderosa pine mixed with oak thickets and some junipers make this a unit where deer herds can drift from south to north as the winter advances.

Unit 6 has high country in the north, then juniper, oak, and grassland as it slopes toward the Verde River Valley. You can hunt from open juniper country to the timberline in Unit 7, the area surrounding the San Francisco Peaks. Good mule deer bucks come from the thick aspen forest on the slopes of these highest of Arizona mountains.

Unit 8 takes in the country south of Williams and is mostly tall pines. The area just south of Grand Canyon National Park is Unit 9, where pines give way to junipers and then open grassland. Unit 10 is lonesome country: no major highways and no settlements except an occasional ranch. All three of these units do have some dandy bucks, especially in areas where pine and juniper meet.

The country north of Prescott, comprising Units 17A and B is a big favorite with deer hunters, and 17B, especially, offers a good chance for success. The country is mostly pine clad, with some mixed pine and juniper.

Unit 19A covers the bulk of Mingus Mountain, a huge chunk of country that always has lots of permits and lots of hunters. Though many deer hunters stick to the higher elevations on Mingus, some of the best deer come from the lower foothills, where cover thins out and the big bucks like to hide. There are enough hunters moving in the thick cover on the mountain so finding a point and waiting for a deer to come by is not a bad strategy. Unit 19B is antelope country and offers hunters mostly juniper cover.

Elk Hunting

A variety of permits are available in this region for archery, muzzleloader, and standard firearms hunters. Seasons are early and late, and some of the units are subdivided. All this intense management is designed to harvest just the number of animals desired and keep elk herds at optimum levels. Some of the fine tuning doesn't work, but generally there are about as many elk as the habitat will support. The yearly fall hunt usually offsets the annual increase.

Units 5, 6, 7, 8, and 9 have elk. Unit 6A has the most permits and is the area where the most elk are taken. The biggest hurdle is getting drawn for a permit. Once in the field, depending a little on which hunt and season, chances of success vary from seven to seventy percent.

Antelope Hunting

This is the heart of Arizona antelope country. The pronghorn is uniquely American, found only on this continent. Because the slim, graceful animals spend their lives in open country, nature has equipped them with blazing speed, perfect camouflage, and keen eyesight. If you drive some of the back country roads in this region, especially early or late in the day, you may find a herd of antelope pacing your vehicle, running effortlessly alongside at more than fifty miles per hour. Their light buff and white color tends to make them disappear when they lie down in the grass or sage flats. Their eyes are placed so they can see in a wide arc, rather than merely straight ahead. Those large eyes are equivalent to eight-power binoculars, so usually when you see an antelope—even through a powerful spotting scope—it has seen you first, and your first view is of an alert animal staring you straight in the eye from a distance of half a mile. Finding antelope in your hunt unit is not usually difficult; the tough part is stalking close enough for a sure shot.

Only Units 20A and 20B do not have antelope hunts. All other units in this region include the kind of open grass and sagebrush habitat favored by the pronghorns.

Unit 10 offers the highest number of permits, and Units 17B and 19B are lumped together in one hunt. The number of permits is high here, too. Because antelope inhabit open country, they are easy to find, and success ratios are usually above fifty percent. In some of the smaller, more restricted hunts, success occasionally is one hundred percent.

Turkey Hunting

Units 5, 6, and 8 are the most popular turkey hunting areas during the annual October season, with 5B getting more hunters than any other single area in the state. The pine forests ring with the calls of hunters trying to fool turkeys, and sometimes all that is attracted is another hunter. As proof of the general wariness of this most American of game birds, success figures usually hover around ten percent. Hunter numbers are unrestricted during the fall, so you need only to have the proper hunting license and tag. You may choose your own spot to hunt.

The spring turkey hunt, for bearded turkeys only, is a permit affair. Unit 6A has the most permits, but Units 5, 7, 8, 9, and 17 also have permits. The hunts are layered: a week of hunting is scheduled for a certain number of participants; then the woods are empty for a few days, and a second hunt begins. This allows fewer hunters in an area at one time and generally contributes to a better quality hunt. The spring turkey chasers don't do much better than their fall counterparts. Success figures are twenty to twenty-five percent.

Javelina Hunting

This region is not a hot spot for javelina distribution. Permits are offered in Units 6A, 19A and 20A and B but relatively few animals are taken except in the latter two. Even so, success figures are generally better than average, perhaps reflecting local hunters with better knowledge. Some 500 javelina are taken here, out of a statewide total of 8,000-plus annually.

Buffalo Hunting

Arizona was too far south to be part of the West's buffalo range, but animals were imported here around the turn of the century. There are currently two herds under the jurisdiction of the Arizona Game and Fish Department. A hunt is held each fall, designed to crop the annual increase and to keep the herds in balance with the available food.

Raymond Ranch, between Flagstaff and Winslow, is home to one of the herds. Less than fifty buffalo are taken here each year, and hunters are chosen by drawing. Only Arizona residents are allowed to participate. There's a one-in-a-lifetime limit, and permits are in the $250-to-$750 range.

Lion and Bear Hunting

Unit 6A is the top bear-hunting area in this region, but bears also are found in 6B, 8, and 19A. About ten percent of the statewide harvest of 200 to 250 bears are taken from this region each year, most with packs of hounds.

Top units for mountain lions in this region are 10 and 17, but a few are taken each year from 5, 6, 7, 8, 9, and 19.

Statewide takes of lions average about 220 per year. This area accounts for about sixty of that number, and about three-fourths of those are taken with dogs.

Small-Game Hunting

The ponderosa pine country that runs from the eastern edge of this region to Williams, the forested areas of Mingus Mountain, and the district north of Prescott are all favorite **squirrel**-hunting haunts. The Abert, or tassel-eared squirrel, is the most popular, and the October season is a perfect time to be in the woods.

Bandtail pigeons love acorns. If there's a good crop of acorns during the October season, the oak thickets will draw huge concentrations of these migratory birds. Units 6A, 9, and 19A are good bets. All the oak-pine areas have some pigeons, although they can be around one day and gone the next while heading for Mexico to spend the winter.

Quail-hunting success depends on bird numbers, which are closely tied to the winter-spring moisture that governs mating and nesting success. In good years, there is excellent hunting in the units with lower elevations. In that category are Units 20A, 20B and the lower one-fourth of 19A. You'll find Gambel's quail here, the top-knotted species so familiar to Arizona residents.

Some **waterfowl** hunting occurs on the lakes and ponds south of Flagstaff early in the season, and there is season-long action along the Verde River for those wanting to reach out-of-the-way places. Shooting on desert tanks and ponds is fairly successful during the latter half of the hunting season. **Rabbit** hunting is best in the more temperate units and very good along washes and brushy banks in Units 20A and 20B. There are some fair to good **dove** flights around desert waterholes, but you should scout in advance which waterholes are being used.

Hunting on horseback is a western tradition.
Val Stannard

Region 4

The Mogollon Rim

At some point in the dim geological past, millions of years ago, the earth's crust shifted abruptly upward to form a cliff face hundreds of miles long and more than 1000 feet higher than the landscape below. Although time has softened some of its features, this fault remains. It is called the Mogollon Rim, and nowhere is its majesty more evident than in the area north and east of the community of Payson.

The huge bulk of the Rim dominates the view from State Route 260 as it winds through the juniper and pine forest from Payson to the resort areas of Kohl's Ranch and Christopher Creek. As the asphalt climbs on up the steep wall of the Rim itself, your attention is drawn from the roadway to the sheer, dark cliff to your left and the steadily increasing drop-off to the right.

When the road finally delivers you on top of the plateau, you stop, partly to celebrate being in one piece, and partly to walk to the Rim's edge and gaze out over hundreds of square miles of soft, green countryside. Sometimes your mind has difficulty accepting what your eyes see. Below the Rim, ridge after ridge rolls away until, on the skyline, the jagged peaks of the Pinal, Mazatzal, and Sierra Ancha ranges loom up. Here, everything relates to the Rim.

The plateau is generally highest where the escarpment falls away. From the edge, the plateau backs away and slopes northward to grassland and the Painted Desert. The slope has spawned many rugged canyons. The top of the Rim from Heber to Long Valley, for example, consists of a series of ridge lines and steep canyon walls.

The same sort of thing happens, on a somewhat smaller scale, below the Rim. Here, debris of a hundred millenniums creates a gentler slope and smaller ridges and canyons.

Atop the Rim are thick forests of spruce, fir, and aspen, crowding close to narrow roads. As the land slants away to the north, great stands of giant ponderosa pine rule, and oak groves appear here and there, until the land drops enough to allow for junipers.

Below the Rim, juniper and manzanita mix with pine, oak, and maple, and sycamores are scattered along the streams down toward Payson.

The old Rim Road, Forest Road 300, winds along the top of the Rim from Woods Canyon Lake to the blissful pavement of State Route 87 north of Strawberry, a distance of forty miles or so. The road is unpaved and inclined to be bumpy but suitable for any sort of vehicle if the driver is not in a hurry and weather conditions are good.

In fact, people in a hurry shouldn't bother to go to the Rim country at all. Drive these back roads early or late in the day, and you may see deer, elk, turkey, and, if you're far enough north, antelope. Sometimes summer visitors, driving slowly down a forest two-track, come upon a herd of elk. Some of the animals will flee one way, some another. But the elk calves separated from their mothers won't go far, nor will the worried females. The forest rings with bawls and barks until the family is reunited.

The Rim Road usually is closed by deep snows from mid-November to about mid-April or early May. During the summer months, it has a lot of traffic. But in spite of the 1.5 million people in the Greater Phoenix area, only two hours away from the cool, 7500-foot elevations, it's still possible to escape the crowds.

That is perhaps the most outstanding feature of the Rim. Walk two hundred yards from any of the unpaved roads atop the Rim, and the sounds of traffic will disappear. The forest area will look the way it looked when the Apache slipped up out of the Tonto Basin to hide in the silent canyons and the first cattle and sheep men used the sunny meadows for summer range.

Until the 1950s, there were no fishing lakes on the Rim, only some natural sinks that held water in the spring but often were dry by fall. The Arizona Game and Fish Department then began an ambitious program and constructed six lakes over the next decade. The seventh, Blue Ridge Reservoir, was built by the Phelps Dodge Corporation.

As it turned out, none of the lakes is as rich as the Game and Fish Department hoped, because none contains enough nutrients to produce good crops of trout. Consequently, most are stocked periodically with eight- to nine-inch trout to supplement earlier stockings of fingerling trout, which grow slowly.

Even so, the Rim lakes are very popular with anglers from late spring to late fall. Fishermen who relish getting away to lightly fished areas can plunge off into one of the deep, steep-walled canyons to take wild trout from the tiny streams. On most trips the satisfaction of getting away is greater than catching any trout.

Contrasts are strong here. The Rim contains both the most and the least visited places: paved highways and dim Indian trails, resorts for those who do not care to explore and rewards for those who do. The Rim's secret canyons and lordly views were immortalized by Zane Grey in a dozen books, but each visitor writes his own novel — titled simply *Memories.*

(Right) A trophy bull elk is king of the forest. The area atop the Mogollon Rim is home to some of the state's largest herds. Judd Cooney

(Left) Bear Canyon Lake is regularly stocked with ''put and take'' trout. Anglers do well from the bank or in a boat. Tony Mandile

(Right) In spite of all the modern tackle available, sometimes the best fishing pole is the old-fashioned tree branch. Some kids are happiest with a little line and a safety pin. Tony Mandile

(Below) Trolling for trout. Dick Dietrich

(Following panel, pages 64-65) Woods Canyon Lake is the Rim's most popular trout-fishing hole. Bob Clemenz

(Above) A nice mess of rainbow trout—the fish most often caught by Rim country anglers. Robert Campbell

(Right) Tonto Creek begins as a spring just below the Rim, flows through an area of summer cabins, resorts, and campgrounds, then plunges into some of the most remote country in the state. Dick Dietrich

(Below) Water pumped from Blue Ridge Reservoir over the Rim into the East Verde River has made a good trout stream from what was a "sometimes" watercourse. Dick Dietrich

(Following panel, pages 68-69) A braggin' size rainbow. Fish this big aren't common on the Rim; most are of the eight- to nine-inch, recently stocked variety. James Tallon

(Left) The Mogollon Rim is both a place and a state of mind. It is one of the most popular fishing and hunting areas in the state, and the outdoorsman finds both mesas and canyons—the easy and the difficult. David Muench

(Below) While the Rim country is only a two-hour drive from the desert heat of Phoenix, the 7000-foot elevation makes for cool nights and pleasant moments around the campfire. Dick Dietrich

(Bottom) One of man's best friends, an English springer spaniel. Tony Mandile

(Far left) November means deer hunting in the Rim country, and a big, beautiful mule deer like this is the reason. James Tallon

(Left) Using a dog for Gambel's quail in the grassland north of the Rim will heighten hunting enjoyment and mean more birds. James Tallon

(Center left) Tall ponderosa pines atop the Rim hold the state's best population of Abert squirrels. Robert Campbell

(Below) The cottontail remains one of the most popular game animals with Arizona hunters. Paul Berquist

(Following panel, pages 74-75) Black bears are rugged, furtive beasts that inhabit a broad area of the Mogollon Rim highlands from central Arizona eastward to the New Mexico border. Larry Toschik

Region 4

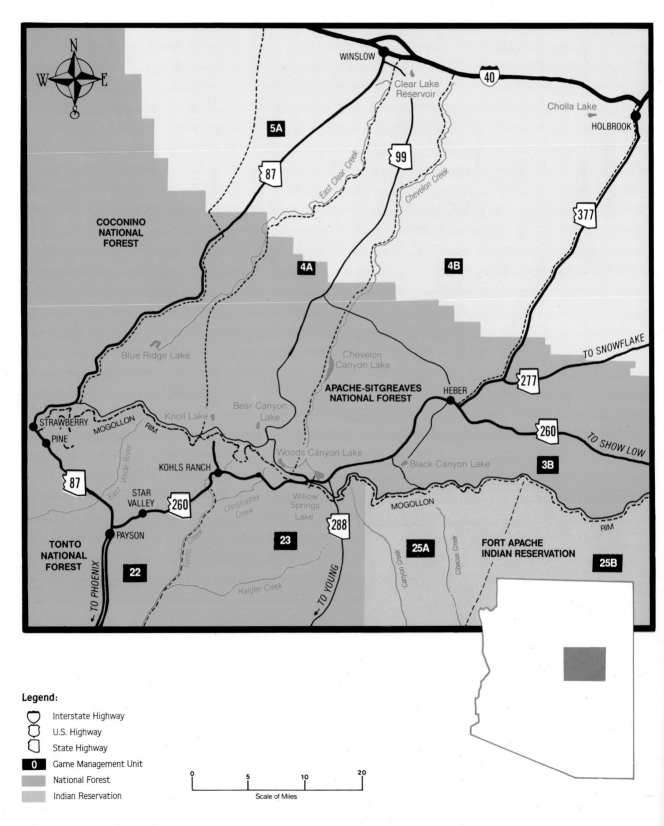

Legend:

- Interstate Highway
- U.S. Highway
- State Highway
- **0** Game Management Unit
- National Forest
- Indian Reservation

0   5   10   20
Scale of Miles

Fishing the Mogollon Rim

Fishing on the Mogollon Rim offers great contrasts. You can be shoulder-to-shoulder with fellow trout fans on the shores of Woods Canyon or Willow Springs lakes, or hike into one of the deep, steep-sided canyons, catch wild trout, and be completely alone for a week.

Because the area is the closest high country fishing-camping opportunity for metropolitan Phoenix, it receives tremendous numbers of visitors, especially during the summer months. Arizona Game and Fish Department hatchery trucks make regular visits to some lakes and streams from May to September, but it's almost impossible to keep up with the demand. Even so, most anglers will catch at least a few rainbow or brown trout despite the fierce competition, and early spring and late fall fishing can be excellent.

Fishing may be better in other parts of the state, but as a place to fish, the Rim has no equal in Arizona.

The Rim Lakes

All lakes on the Rim that hold fish are man-made. The natural lakes can vary from several feet deep when filled with snow melt in the spring to a weedy bog by fall and are too undependable to stock with fish. Construction of the seven lakes atop the Rim began in the late 1950s, and all were built in the next ten years.

Woods Canyon was the first man-made lake on the Rim and is still the most popular: fifty acres of blue in the tall pines and aspen. It is just off the top of the Rim on State Route 260, then four miles west on the paved access road. Some of the rainbow trout here are stocked as "catchables," that is, eight- to nine-inch fish direct from the hatchery; others are planted as smaller fish and allowed to grow with Mother Nature providing the food. There is a store with boat rental, and a boat can be helpful. You can prospect sections of the shoreline that are lightly fished, and trolling with "Cowbell" flashers followed by a worm or wet fly is always a good bet. Shore fishermen, using bait, account for the majority of Woods Canyon fish. Those who use very light leaders fool more trout.

Ice fishing is popular with those who fancy the hike in from Route 260. There's always some good action just after the ice goes out in early spring. A free boat-launch ramp is available, but the lake is restricted to electric motors only. The campground here is as popular as the lake.

Willow Springs lies one paved mile off State Route 260. You'll hit the turnoff approximately one mile east of the Woods Canyon road. There's a paved launch ramp with parking lot, but motors are limited to eight horsepower. Willow Springs has rainbows and brown trout and is infested with golden shiner minnows, illegally stocked. Largemouth bass were also illegally introduced into the lake.

They eat the shiners (and trout) but bass to two or three pounds are occasionally caught. Both the shiners and the bass compete with trout and may eventually crowd them out. Brown trout have been stocked to prey on the shiners, and the potential for huge brown trout is very real. Browns as big as seven or eight pounds are taken here every year. Chevelon Canyon and Woods Canyon lakes also suffer the shiner blight.

At 150 acres, Willow Springs is one of the larger Rim lakes, and fishing is generally a bit better here than at other Rim waters. Shore fishing is most popular along the lake near the parking area and on down toward the dam. Use a boat to fish the deeper parts of the lake during the summer months, with lures or bait, or try the area near the inlet stream late in the fall for spawning browns. Most fish taken year-round are rainbows. Ice fishing (walk in) is safe during most winters.

Black Canyon Lake holds rainbows and browns. The seventy-eight-acre lake is six miles south of State Route 260 on an unpaved road. Access is sometimes muddy and slick in the rainy season, and the lake is locked up by snow during the winter months. You'll find a large paved parking area, restrooms, and a paved launch ramp.

Most fishing is done from the bank with bait, and rainbows, mostly seven to eight inches, are the bulk of the catch. Trollers and boat fishermen using bait in deep water take most of the larger brown trout. Only electric motors are allowed. The shoreline of Black Canyon is open enough for fly fishing, and the last hour of the day is a good time to try black or brown wooly worm flies. The trout also relish wet flies during summer rain showers.

Chevelon Canyon Lake takes some extraordinary effort just to get to the shore. Access is from Winslow via Forest Roads 504 and 169, or take 169 north from the Rim Road about five miles west of Woods Canyon. Chevelon is deep in the canyon of the same name, and its 200 acres wind through the steep walls for three miles or so.

When the Game and Fish Department put an earthen dam in a narrow part of the canyon to form the lake, the first job was building a narrow road down the canyonside. Since the lake was completed back in the mid-1960s, the road has slowly deteriorated and is now closed completely, so the lake is a walk-in. The old road is about a mile long; there's a shorter foot trail at the upper end of the lake.

A boat is useful here and outboards to eight horsepower are permitted. Fishing at Chevelon is limited to flies and lures only — no bait. There's also a "slot" limit. That means you must release all trout between 10 and 14 inches, and if you decide to keep a fish as part of your limit, it must be killed at once.

Rainbows and browns are the catches, and a Payson angler landed a fourteen-pound, five-ounce brown trout here in February 1984. Early spring and fall months are best

Fishing

for all fish, and the biggies definitely hit better then. Those big browns will hit a fly, and lures work well here, too. It's never crowded. A six trout possession limit is in force and all fish must be at least 14" in length.

Bear Canyon is relatively free of angling pressure for a variety of reasons. The first is an "artificial lures only" rule. This means artificial flies or hardware — no bait allowed. Second, you must walk down a steep hill to the lake, although there is an excellent trail. And, last, trees grow right down to the edge of the water, so fly-fishing from shore can mean more bites from pinetree branches than rainbows.

That hill keeps out most boaters, but a light canoe or inflatable boat carries you into open water where casting is possible. The lake is one of the prettiest on the Rim, about sixty acres, and located two miles north of Forest Road 300 (the Rim Road) at a junction about nine miles west of Woods Canyon.

You may use an electric motor on Bear Canyon, although it's hard to imagine anybody wanting to carry a motor and battery up and down that trail. Wet flies and nymph patterns work well, as do spinning lures. Rainbows make up most of the catch. You may occasionally take a brook trout from earlier stockings. Warning: the no-bait rule is strictly enforced. That angler next to you may be an undercover Game and Fish Department ranger.

Knoll is best fished from a boat. You can pull ashore with some chilled wine and cheese for lunch on the pine-dotted rocky island, which gives this little jewel its name. The lake is just seventy-five acres but seems larger because of two arms that stretch back into the timber. There's a parking lot with an unpaved boat launch near the dam.

Using a boat is an excellent way to work the unfished shoreline away from the parking lot and campground. Only electric motors are allowed. Trolling is a good bet, and so is fly-fishing the weed beds in the shallows at the upper ends of both arms of the lake. There are mostly rainbows here, but some big browns live in the lake, too. A 12-pounder was taken in 1983 by a lady angler from Mesa. As is true with other Arizona trout waters, early spring and late fall are the top times.

Blue Ridge was built as a payback by Phelps Dodge to replace water taken out of Black River for Morenci mining operations. Blue Ridge gives Arizona fishermen two benefits: It provides a lake, and the water pumped out of the lake and over the Rim into the East Verde River transforms that stream — previously just a trickle — into a good trout-fishing river.

There is a drawback. Blue Ridge is in the bottom of a narrow, steep-sided canyon; it is scenic but limited in access. There is a long launch ramp and motors to eight horsepower are permitted, but only a few foot trails lead from the road down to the water's edge.

About the only way to fish most of the lake is from a boat,

so try trolling the shady sides of the canyon walls with a spinning lure; or let the boat drift and fish with bait deep in the same areas. Bait seems to be the best bet from shore. Look for rainbows and perhaps an occasional brown trout (including some lunkers).

There are seventy acres twisting in a giant "U" shape from the dam. The lake is about six miles east of State Route 87 off an unpaved but good road. The turnoff from Route 87 is four and a half miles north of Clint's Well. Rock Crossing campground serves the area. It's about halfway between Blue Ridge and Route 87.

Clear Creek Reservoir, about sixty acres confined by the walls of Clear Creek Canyon, is just southeast of Winslow. There is parking, with a launch ramp; no motor restrictions on the lake. Trout are stocked (mostly rainbows), and the lake also contains some remnant populations of bass, plus catfish. Although there's always a chance of a good trout carried over from previous stocks, this is a family fishing lake, and the small fish are appreciated.

Cholla lies just off Interstate Route 40 about eleven miles west of Holbrook. The 360-acre lake is the water storage for the power plant nearby. Heated water is returned to the lake, so there is abundant weed growth. Fishing is for warm water species, mainly catfish and some bass. A "slot" limit here requires anglers to release all bass between 12 and 16 inches. There is a launch area; no motor restrictions.

(Far right) Tonto Creek, the "mother" trout stream below the Rim, gathers a dozen tributaries as it flows toward Roosevelt Lake and the Salt River. Jerry Jacka

(Below) Conserving energy, a fisherman takes his ease while waiting for a bite. Don B. Stevenson

Rim Country Streams

Streams here are small to very small. The easily accessible waters are stocked from early May to after the Labor Day weekend with eight- to nine-inch rainbow trout and most are caught by anglers in the following week. The remote streams, especially those in deep canyons, are lightly fished and contain so-called "wild trout" — meaning they are stream-hatched, sometimes for several generations. In the very smallest streams, trout live only in pools, the connecting trickle being too shallow. A large trout in this kind of environment is a fish of eight inches.

Tonto Creek is crossed by State Route 260 sixteen miles northeast of Payson, and the waters here are stocked during the summer months with rainbow trout. There are remote, hike-in stretches downstream where Haigler Creek enters Tonto. Occasionally, trout in the twelve- to eighteen-inch class are taken from these areas. There are two campgrounds on the creek, just upstream from Kohl's Ranch.

Christopher Creek access is twenty-four miles northeast of Payson on Route 260. Christopher Creek is stocked near the campground during the summer months with rainbow trout. There is some good fishing upstream from the resorts and up and downstream from the campground. The catch is mostly pan-size trout.

Canyon Creek is Arizona's nod to quality fishing, and this small stream is reserved for fly-fishing and lure-fishing only from its source under the Rim to the border of the Fort Apache Indian Reservation. Take Forest Road 188 off State Route 288 — the Young Road. The creek is stocked with rainbow trout, and occasional brown trout are caught as well. There is about five miles of fishable water. Small, well-dressed flies in black or brown will catch fish for the patient, careful angler.

Haigler Creek is reached by driving south of State Route 260 on Forest Road 291 and 200. There is fishing up and downstream from the road crossing. Stocked sporadically during the summer, as water flow and temperatures permit, the creek is lightly fished, especially downstream where it flows in a deepening canyon. Access is difficult. Except for rainbows and browns, anything over twelve inches is a lunker for a stream this small.

Under-the-Rim streams are a group of tiny streams that begin at the base of the Mogollon Rim and flow for a few miles before joining other, larger waters. Pine, Webber, Dude, Ellison, Horton, Chase, and Bonita creeks are found between the town of Pine and Tonto Creek, where Horton empties. All are very small, jump-across creeks, and the fish — mostly rainbows and brook trout — match the water. A six- or seven-inch trout is a trophy. These are stream-hatched trout; wild, vividly colored slices of the Arizona outdoors. These streams are for patient walkers only.

East Verde River was improved as a trout stream with the building of Blue Ridge Reservoir. Water from Blue Ridge is pumped over the Rim into the stream each summer, and the added flow makes the river a major trout stream in the area. The stream is accessible in a number of spots in the area north of Payson, including a crossing on Forest Road 64, which parallels the Rim; and from Forest Road 199, the Houston Mesa Road. Stocked with rainbows during the summer months, the stream is best in May and June when the water is still high and cold.

Chevelon Creek runs from the top of the Rim at Woods Canyon Lake, through steep Chevelon Canyon to the lake of the same name, then downstream for many miles to its junction with the Little Colorado east of Winslow. It's a fair-sized stream, but brushy and hard to fish. There are rainbows and brown trout, including some trophy fish. A few dim trails lead down into the canyon that holds the stream, but this is remote, wild country, not to be tackled without thorough preparation. The best fishing is between Woods Canyon and Chevelon Canyon lakes.

East Clear Creek is approached by Forest Roads 211 and 95 below Blue Ridge Reservoir and at Mack's Crossing on Forest Road 137, several miles downstream. There is some stocking of eight- to nine-inch rainbow trout at these sites, but the rest of the creek contains wild, stream-hatched trout, both rainbow and brown. Flows sometimes go underground in parts of the canyon that contain the stream, but at some bends in the canyon there always are pools of water with fish. The area is very rugged and remote and suitable only for well-equipped walkers.

Atop-the-Rim streams are small and not stocked and are always in deep canyons with little or no access. Dude, Dane, Barbershop, Miller, and Leonard below Knoll Lake all fit in this category. The fish, usually rainbows or browns, are small, and the going is tough.

Hunting the Mogollon Rim

The Rim country offers good hunting for deer, elk, antelope, and turkey, plus some small game. There are pockets of whitetail deer habitat just under the Rim to go with the mule deer that live throughout the area. Elk hunting atop the Rim varies from good to excellent, and it is one of the most popular turkey-hunting areas. And where the pines begin to thin and juniper-grassland takes over in the northern part of the units, there is excellent hunting for antelope. There are bear and lion here, too, although neither appears in substantial numbers.

The open, parklike ponderosa pine forests hold good squirrel populations, and if you're in the right place at the right time, bandtail pigeons can provide fast action. Waterfowl hunting is limited to the stock ponds and occasional marshy "lakes" but can be very good early in the season.

The good hunting in the Rim country is the result of startling changes in habitat that can occur from the edge of the Rim at 7500 to 8000 feet northward to the grassland at 4800 feet. This is one of the most popular hunting areas in Arizona with the deep canyons and thickly forested ridges, the dense juniper and manzanita thickets, and the oak-filled draws and big patches of roadless country.

Deer Hunting

Both **Rocky Mountain mule deer** and the smaller **Coues whitetail deer** abound here. The whitetails are found mostly in the area directly under the Rim from the head of Tonto Creek east to Canyon Creek, and there are some scattered populations atop the Rim as well. Mule deer are found throughout the area.

The statewide average success on deer is twenty to twenty-five percent and Game Management Units 4A, 4B, and 5A, which cover the area atop the Rim, usually fall within that range. Early snows may push deer out of the high country toward the junipers, but generally the good places to hunt for deer are in small draws with oak or aspen thickets, in rims and side canyons of deeper drainages, and in stands of cliffrose. The Rim country is full of old burns —areas that have suffered forest fires in the past and are now in some stage of regrowth. These are favorites of deer and elk, especially during early or late hours of the day.

Most hunters stick to the easy-to-hunt flats, reluctant to dive off into some of the rough canyon country. But the breaks and rimrock hold the good bucks, and if you commit yourself to some extra effort, the odds begin to swing in your favor.

Antelope Hunting

The grassland and juniper country on the north end of Units 4 and 5 is antelope habitat. This swift plains animal will never be widespread in our state, and each herd is carefully managed to keep it within the limits of the avail-able living space and food supply. Figure on about 50 total permits for these two areas and more than 500 applicants.

Unit 4B generally has the most permits, but if you're lucky enough to get a permit anywhere in the Rim country, your odds for success are better than eighty percent. Don't skip the juniper areas; the breaks, meadows, and canyons often are as good as the wide open spaces farther north toward Interstate 40.

Elk Hunting

The Merriam's elk that was native to Arizona disappeared about the turn of the century. In 1913, the Elks Lodge in Winslow imported a small herd of elk from Wyoming and that transplant, along with other introductions, has grown to the current estimated population of 15,000 to 20,000 elk in our state.

Elk once were plains animals, but now they inhabit the broad band of timber country that sweeps across the middle of the state from the White Mountains to Flagstaff and Williams.

The modern hunt is divided into several archery and firearms seasons, some early (September), others during November. Some hunts are for bulls only. A limited number of antlerless elk permits are issued, and one early hunt is for trophy bulls only. This mix of seasons and hunts lets the greatest number of hunters participate while still achieving the management goals of keeping elk numbers in balance with the habitat and food supply.

Generally, Units 4A, 4B, and 5A atop the Rim offer better hunting and higher success than Units 22 and 23, just under the Rim. Odds on getting drawn for elk vary from even for archery-bull hunts to twenty-five-to-one for trophy hunts.

Turkey Hunting

All five of the Rim country hunt units offer spring turkey hunts. These are for bearded turkey only, and that normally means males or gobblers, which have a "beard" of coarse black hair that hangs from the middle of the breast. But hen turkeys occasionally sport the beard, too, and the Game and Fish Department figures it's too much to expect an excited hunter to tell the difference between a hen and a gobbler.

The spring hunts are by permit only and take place in April and May, about the time the gobblers are looking for hens and are thus a bit less wary than usual. Hunters use artificial calls to challenge the strutting gobblers, who are jealous of their harems and are sometimes so combative they will charge a pickup if it stops on a back road and the horn is honked.

An "any turkey" hunt is held in October, but there is no drawing. Hunters with a hunting license simply buy a tag, head for the woods, and hunt anywhere they like. The Rim country is one of the favorite spots for fall turkey hunters, with Units 4A and 5A drawing the most hunters. Success varies from year to year, with turkey population closely tied to spring moisture. But fifteen percent is a long-term average and the five units that make up the Rim country are always close to that figure.

Turkeys operate as a flock, and if a bunch is scattered, it's not much of a trick to use an artificial call to lure some of them within range.

Bear Hunting

All Arizona bears are black bears, even though they may range in color from dark brown to blond. There were a few grizzly bears in the state historically but they disappeared many years ago. The black bear is such a shy, retiring creature that even though Arizona has a fair population of the bruins, it's possible to spend a lifetime camping, fishing, and hiking in the Arizona back country without seeing one of them. Hunting, especially without dogs, is very tough. In fact, the best chance to spot a bear may be around a campground in the summer months, when they become addicted to the easy food supplies in campground garbage cans. A number of bears are taken each fall by deer or elk hunters who have bought a bear tag "just in case" but who are not afield with bear as their primary concern. Aside from following a pack of hounds, the best bet for hunters is using a predator call, which, under the right conditions, can bring a bear well within rifle or bow range. In spite of oft-told campfire tales of black bears that weigh over 500 pounds, the average is probably half that.

Though the parts of Units 22 and 23 that are included in the Rim region do have bears in residence, it is the areas farther south — treated in a different chapter — that hold the bulk of the bear population in these units. Hunting atop the Rim is best in Unit 5B, a thickly forested area with extremely rugged canyons. A few bears come from Unit 4B. The short season here is in late September. Most bears are taken with dogs.

Lion Hunting

Few lions are taken in these units. Early winter is the best hunting time, and nearly all the lions also are taken with the aid of dogs.

Small-Game Hunting

Abert squirrels are the most prevalent here, and spending an October day in the ponderosa pines chasing squirrels is one of fall's genuine pleasures. The season opens in early October and runs to mid-November. Many hunters take squirrels incidentally while in the woods on some other mission, but they are worth a hunt all on their own.

A scope-sighted .22 rifle is perfect. Calm, sunny days are best, and look for squirrels on the ground in open parks of ponderosa or in oak thickets in years of good acorn crops. The daily bag limit is five squirrels.

Bandtail pigeon: This is a migratory bird, with federal rules and seasons, and some or most of the birds may fly south before the October season begins along the Rim. Bandtails love to congregate in the tops of dead pines, and they are easy to spot when the flocks choose that kind of roost. They also love acorns, and there are many oaks along the Rim. If you can find areas that have small water impoundments and oak trees with acorns, bandtails are likely to be around. Small side canyons off major drainages are good places to check as well. Areas just under the Rim can hold good numbers of birds, too. Try to do some pre-season scouting.

Waterfowl: The Rim country is not a duck-goose hot spot. However, there is some hunting along the major creeks and on some of the marshy "lakes," especially in the more open country in the northern part of Units 4 and 5 early in the season, before the freeze occurs.

Rabbit: There is good rabbit hunting in the juniper-sage-grassland in the northern part of Units 4 and 5. Check brushy draws, along creek bottoms, and in areas where tumbles of rock occur in good grass cover. The season is open year-round, and almost any sort of gun or bow and arrow is legal. The daily bag limit is ten.

Abert squirrel

The White Mountains

You can feel the serenity of the White Mountains in the spring, when snowbanks linger along the road from Pinetop to Big Lake and you're the only angler to enjoy the chill wind that blows off the high peaks. Springtime freshets, hustling to an appointment with mother stream, crisscross the landscape, hiding drinks in secret places for the summer flowers that will follow.

Summer is the busy time, as desert dwellers trek to these highlands to trade saguaro cacti for spruce trees and to cut the temperature in half. Even so, serenity is just off the main highway, two minutes' drive down some side road, where you can spend a week alone. It rains nearly every day in July and August; short, sharp, chilly showers that wash the landscape clean, banish the dust from unpaved roads, and provide a perfect excuse for an afternoon nap.

There may be patches of snow still gleaming on Mount Baldy or Mount Ord in July — both reach elevations of more

than 11,000 feet. And even at 9000 feet, early morning temperatures sometimes turn dew to frost. It's difficult for Phoenix residents to remember this when packing clothes for a weekend visit and it's 110 degrees outside. The White Mountains do warm up during the day, of course, sometimes to the 80s. If you spend a few hours on the water fishing for trout, you'll probably get a sunburn along with your limit of rainbows.

Autumn is serene in the White Mountains, too. School starts, and the summer-vacation crowds migrate back to desert communities. By late September, aspen trees at the highest elevations begin their magic change from soft green to yellow and gold. And as October advances, the color spills down the mountainsides like celestial honey. There are other performers in the great color show, but none more spectacular than the aspens when they arch over dusty logging roads and turn them into golden tunnels.

Fishing livens up in the fall. Trout feed almost frantically,

sensing the need to store energy for the long winter ahead. The time from mid-October to the end of November, when ice locks up high lakes and snow closes roads, is often the best of all for dedicated trout fans. Rainbows, brookies, browns, and cutthroats, fattened by the feasts of summer, are in the mood to do battle, and many a complacent angler stands shaken after a broad-shouldered trout has left him with a broken leader and the glimpse of a huge dorsal fin.

Fall months are also prime hunting time, and if you're lucky, you can combine turkey with trout, deer with ducks, or bear with brook trout.

Although most campgrounds are closed, many people choose the fall for camping, claiming a patch of timber on the edge of a meadow for their very own — at least for a few days — and relishing the clean, sweet, sunny days and the chilly nights that are ideal for sleeping. Crisp November mornings are almost impossible to describe, even to another hunter. But the aroma of coffee perking and bacon frying, as you fumble into a heavy coat, is one of life's genuine pleasures.

On the high peaks and meadows, the serenity of winter comes early and stays late. Snowplows clear the main roads, keeping villages like Greer and Alpine and the ski slopes at Sunrise accessible. But the country south of State Route 260 and west of U.S. Route 666 generally is one big snowdrift. Only the tracks of an occasional snowmobile or cross-country skier break the cold white surface from late November to late April.

Ice fishing is still a minor sport in Arizona, but a sprinkling of die-hard trout chasers is often in attendance on sunny winter days at Luna Lake or Tunnel Lake at Greer. Snowmobilers do well at Big and Crescent. "In town" lakes like Rainbow and Show Low, where access is no problem, usually do not have safe ice.

Yet even the deepest snow eventually melts, and another White Mountain year begins.

(Above left) The West Fork of the Little Colorado begins on the slopes of Mount Baldy, passes beneath the bridge at Sheep's Crossing, then heads through rough country toward Greer. It offers mostly rainbow trout, with a chance at browns. Jerry Sieve

(Right) Tall trees crowding close to the blue water, boats ready for an hour's fishing at dusk, trout big enough to cause stories of broken leaders — all part of the personality of a White Mountain lake. Bob Clemenz

(Left) Mexican Hay Lake appears to be more hay than lake — but it grows big rainbow trout, with fall the prime time to catch them. Dick Dietrich

(Below) Relaxin' and fishin' go together. No sense in getting too excited; the fish will bite when they're ready. Dick Dietrich

(Bottom) This brook trout didn't want to leave the stream. Bob Hirsch

(Following panel, pages 86-87) Crescent Lake's shallow waters are loaded with food, and it grows trout as well as any lake in the area. Dick Dietrich

(Top) A young trout fan tries his luck in the Little Colorado River. Jerry Jacka

(Above) The bridge is over the water and water has fish, so this must be the place. Don B. Stevenson

(Right) The Little Colorado River gets a little bigger after other forks join at Greer, Arizona. Dick Dietrich

Hunter at sunrise. Rick Odell

(Insets) White Mountain game animals: bighorn sheep, antelope, and mule deer.
Tony Mandile

*(Following panel, pages 92-93) The piney mountains of the Navajo reservation,
almost all the Mogollon country, North and South Kaibab, and the "sky island"
forests of southeastern Arizona shelter Merriam's turkeys.* Larry Toschik

Region 5

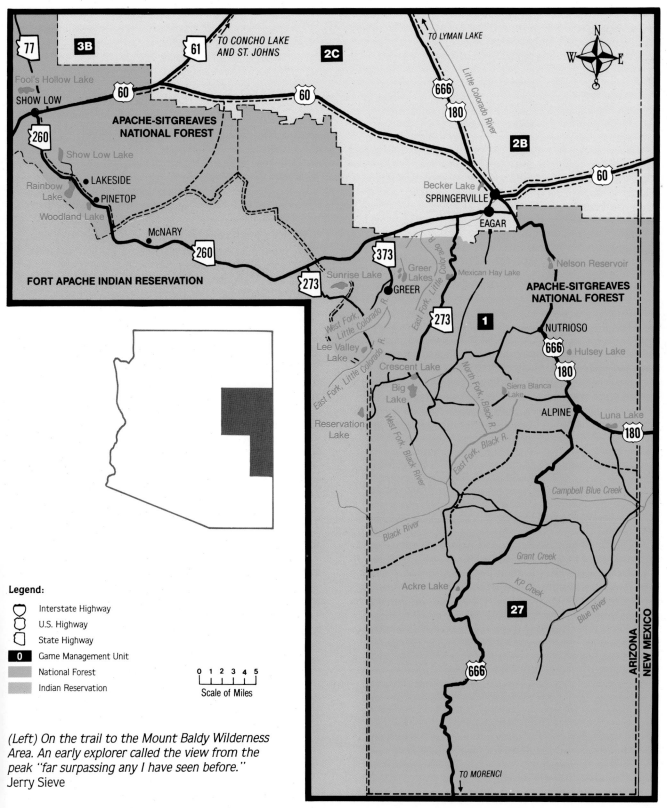

Legend:

	Interstate Highway
	U.S. Highway
	State Highway
0	Game Management Unit
	National Forest
	Indian Reservation

0 1 2 3 4 5
Scale of Miles

(Left) On the trail to the Mount Baldy Wilderness Area. An early explorer called the view from the peak "far surpassing any I have seen before."
Jerry Sieve

Map labels:

77 3B 61 TO CONCHO LAKE AND ST. JOHNS 2C TO LYMAN LAKE N W E S

Fool's Hollow Lake 60 60 666 180 Little Colorado River

SHOW LOW APACHE-SITGREAVES NATIONAL FOREST 2B

260 Show Low Lake Becker Lake SPRINGERVILLE 60

Rainbow Lake LAKESIDE PINETOP EAGAR

Woodland Lake McNARY 260 373 Nelson Reservoir

FORT APACHE INDIAN RESERVATION 273 Sunrise Lake Greer Lakes GREER Mexican Hay Lake APACHE-SITGREAVES NATIONAL FOREST

West Fork, Little Colorado R. East Fork, Little Colorado R. 273 1 NUTRIOSO 666 180 Hulsey Lake

Lee Valley Lake East Fork, Little Colorado R. Crescent Lake North Fork, Black R. Sierra Blanca Lake ALPINE 180 Luna Lake

Big Lake West Fork, Black River East Fork, Black R. Campbell Blue Creek

Reservation Lake Black River Grant Creek

Ackre Lake KP Creek Blue River 27 ARIZONA NEW MEXICO

666 TO MORENCI

95

Fishing the White Mountains

Although trout are not the only fish found in the White Mountains, they are certainly the most popular. Most anglers feel lake fishing is easier and more productive, so let's take a look at the region's trout lakes.

Becker Lake

Becker Lake is special. It's the only body of water in the state with a closed season and this, combined with other regulations, helps the Game and Fish Department manage the 85-acre lake as a trophy trout fishery. The season generally opens in early April and closes the end of November. Depending on water temperatures, the best fishing is in April, May, and early June, and again in October and November.

Becker is not the most scenic lake in the White Mountains, but the trout it holds are big and beautiful. When you catch big fish, you tend to forget the surroundings. Special regulations apply here, designed to keep an excellent population of larger trout in residence. You can catch and release as many fish as you wish but "keepers" must be larger than a stated minimum—fourteen inches, as an example—that may change from year to year. There's a reduced limit to four fish. The idea is to release the smaller fish and give them a chance to grow to braggin' size.

Another rule prohibits live trout on a stringer or in a live well, basket, or similar container; that means if you catch a rainbow or brown trout larger than the legal minimum and decide to keep it as part of your daily limit, it must be killed at once. This keeps unscrupulous fishermen from "high-grading" (releasing smaller fish when bigger ones are caught). Although the released fish may appear frisky and unharmed, no trout held on a stringer or in a basket and handled several times will survive.

Barbless hooks are the easy way to be sure your smaller-than-keeper fish can be released without harm. You can buy barbless flies, or even purchase barbless hooks and tie your own flies. But the easiest way to handle this matter — with either flies or lures — is simply to mash down the barbs with a pair of needle-nose pliers. It isn't necessary to touch a trout you wish to release if it's been caught on a barbless hook. Slide your hand down the line to the hook and flick it out of the trout's jaw. Sometimes the trout will unhook itself before you're ready!

Flyrods are a big favorite at Becker, but you can use a spinning rod and a fly to fool the fish too. Simply pinch a small split shot on the leader about three feet up from the fly, then cast and reel slowly, letting the fly get down deep, just off the bottom. A plastic casting bubble, partially filled with water, will take the fly down in the same fashion and you won't need the split shot.

A boat is a big asset, but shore fishing is okay, and there are some stretches of shoreline where waders are helpful. The lake is restricted to electric motors.

When using flies, fish slowly, just off the bottom. Favorite patterns include wooly worms (all colors); peacock lady and brown hackle peacock; gold-ribbed hare's ear, and nymphs like Ted's stone fly and the Montana nymph.

Facilities include a launch area, parking, and restrooms, but no overnight camping is allowed. The lake is two miles northwest of Springerville off State Route 60. There is a commercial campground along the highway about a half-mile east of the lake.

Big Lake

Big Lake is the undisputed queen of Arizona trout waters. More trout are caught here than at any other single lake in the state. While the lake's 500 acres are not big by most standards, the water is extremely rich, and fishermen take about 400,000 rainbow and brook trout each year. There's never a guarantee in fishing, but Big Lake comes close.

Most of the fish are rainbow trout in the eight- to ten-inch length, so-called pan fish. Chances of hooking a trout in the "teens" is good, and nearly every week, fish of three or four pounds are taken. Big Lake is managed as a family lake, a place where a family can camp and have an excellent chance of catching enough trout for a daily fresh fish dinner.

Since a majority of Big Lake anglers are in the non-expert category, bait is the most popular way to put a trout on the stringer. Live worms, salmon eggs (especially the "fireball" variety), whole-kernel corn, and cheese attract lots of fish. Shore fishermen use bait almost exclusively, and many boaters anchor and fish the same way.

There are periods in late afternoon during the summer months when fly fishermen can work dry flies, but wet patterns are the usual choice, with sink tips or sinking lines needed to get the flies deep. Any well-dressed fly in sizes six to fourteen will catch Big Lake trout. Wooly worms in sizes two to four work well in late summer and early fall.

Spoons and lures get a lot of play here as well, with the long collections of spinners called Ford Fenders, Cowbells, or Lake Trolls being popular. These have no hooks of their own but are trolled as attractors. A hook full of worms trailed two feet behind the spinner rig is widely used, but a small spinning lure like the Z-Ray or Mepps also works, as do wet flies. Spoons and plugs can be cast or trolled.

Big Lake facilities are excellent. The concessionaire gives good advice on where and how to catch fish, and offers rental boats, ice, gas, and propane at a surprisingly well-equipped store. Apache National Forest has a paved boat-launch ramp and adjacent parking, and there's a first class fish-cleaning station not far from the store. Taken as a whole—fishing, facilities, and campground — the Big Lake area can serve as a model on how a recreational complex should be administered.

The lake is about forty miles southeast of Pinetop via State Routes 260 and 273. The last fifteen miles are graded gravel, suitable for any sort of vehicle. Deep snow keeps State Route 273 closed from late November to late April, although those dates may vary a couple of weeks either way, depending on the ferocity of the winter.

Around Greer

Greer lakes is the collective name for Bunch, Tunnel, and River reservoirs, all clustered just a mile or so north of the resort community of Greer.

River Reservoir is stocked with rainbow trout, and thousands are caught each summer, mostly pan-size. But it's the giant brown trout that make River Reservoir's reputation. A fourteen-pounder from here held the state record for many years (until it was beaten by a sixteen-pounder from Horseshoe Cienega Lake on the Fort Apache reservation). Browns that large are very unusual, but good numbers of fish in the three- to six-pound range are taken each year. Fishing in a lake that holds fish that big is a special thrill. There is a boat launch area; only electric motors are allowed on the lake.

Bait catches most of the rainbows, but the browns prefer lures and flies. A Repala lure fooled the sixteen-pounder.

Tunnel Lake also has rainbows and browns, but rainbows get most of the attention. Easy access helps keep this a popular spot and eight- to nine-inch trout are stocked regularly during the summer months.

Boats are a help, but a majority of Tunnel Lake anglers do their thing from shore with bait. The fifteen surface acres mean electric motors only.

Tunnel is within walking distance of paved State Route 373, so it's accessible in the winter months. When temperatures ensure safe ice, Tunnel is a popular spot.

Bunch Lake, like its two partners, is at 8200 feet. It is twenty acres when full, but the level does fluctuate. Fishing for rainbow and brown trout is best from March through May, when the water is still high and cold. You'll catch mostly pan-size fish with the chance of an occasional brown trout to spice the action. Bunch is lightly fished compared with Tunnel and River.

Ackre Lake

Ackre Lake is only two surface acres, and even in water-loving Arizona, you have to strain credulity to hang the "lake" tag on this little pond. It's at the end of a bumpy, winding road in the high pines a few miles south of Hannagan Meadow. Brook trout are stocked each year, and most of the fish caught are pan-size at best. There are only a half-dozen waters in the state that are restricted to lure and/or fly fishing, and Ackre is one of them. Small spinning lures, such as small Z-Rays or "0" size Mepps, will catch brookies, as will flies on fine tippets.

Crescent Lake

Crescent Lake is just north of Big Lake, and the two share a reputation for growing fish fast. But Crescent is much shallower and thus susceptible to fish loss during severe winters. When snow covers the ice for long periods of time and blocks sunlight, weeds die and release carbon dioxide. Oxygen levels plummet, and the lake may lose its entire stock of fish.

Crescent is stocked with rainbow trout each spring and they provide good action all summer and fall, growing from pan-size to the mid-teens in the process. Brook trout, which have a better tolerance for low oxygen levels, normally survive the winters to provide bigger prizes for anglers who hit the lake in early spring; some outlast the summer and reach two to three pounds by fall.

Crescent is shallow and weedy and thus a big favorite with fly fishermen, who particularly like the upper end of the lake. Wet flies, worked low and slow, account for the most fish. Bait and lures are popular as well, and shore anglers account for a good bit of the pressure. There is a small store with boat-rental dock. Outboards to eight horsepower are allowed on Crescent's 100 acres, and at 9000 feet, it's cool even during the summer months. Try Crescent in late October or November until snow closes the road. There aren't as many fish as in summer, but those remaining are bigger and fatter.

Bunch Reservoir, one of the three lakes near Greer. Bunch is best in the spring, when some broad-shouldered brown trout are taken. Bob Clemenz

Fishing

Lee Valley Lake

Lee Valley Lake is one of the most beautiful spots in the White Mountains, tucked away in a quiet corner of the forest at the foot of 11,590-foot Mount Baldy. The thirty-five acre lake contains brook trout and grayling and fishing is restricted to flies and lures only. Grayling must be at least 12 inches long and there is a sharply reduced limit—check this year's regulations. Action here is best in spring and early summer, again in the fall just before freeze-up. Both brookies and grayling love black flies; the peacock-bodied patterns work well too. So do small Z-Rays in silver or gold.

Access is via State Route 273, about halfway between Sunrise and Crescent lakes. There are restrooms, a parking lot, and a paved launch ramp, but no other facilities.

Hulsey Lake (Pond)

Hulsey Lake, it is said, is like love—best in the spring. The three-acre pond is about seven miles north of Alpine off U. S. Route 666. It is stocked with pan-size rainbow trout until the water gets too warm — usually by June. Rig a bobber and a worm, and let the kids catch a few here.

Woodland Reservoir

Woodland Reservoir is a ten-acre "in town" lake, just a couple of blocks from the main street in Pinetop. It tries to be a trout lake, but over the years bass, catfish, and sunfish have found their way in, and trout are generally stocked only in the spring when the water is cold. Woodland is not generally appealing to the serious angler, but offers a good place to keep the kids busy.

Mexican Hay Lake

Mexican Hay Lake has a self-explanatory name: Sometimes it's a lake, sometimes a hay field, because it depends on winter snow melt for its existence. It's about thirty-five acres when full, but even then no more than eight or ten feet deep at best, and the shallower parts of the lake grow thickly with reeds and hay. This shallow, weedy character helps the lake grow trout. If there's sufficient water in the spring, pan-size rainbows are stocked, and they become fourteen to fifteen inches by late fall. When a very mild winter lets some of these fish survive, they can reach three or four pounds by the end of the next season. There are no facilities, and it's tough fishing without a boat. The lake is beside State Route 273 about halfway between Springerville and Crescent Lake.

Concho Lake

Concho Lake is sixty acres of big-fish water off State Route 61 between St. Johns and Show Low. Concho used to be sixty acres of weeds, but is now easily fishable as a result of Jaws III, the Game and Fish Department weed cutter. This is a gigantic machine that cuts weeds six feet below the surface and stores them in a hopper so they can be stacked on shore. Excellent fly fishing exists for rainbow and brook trout, especially during the winter months when Concho seldom freezes. Five-pound fish are not easy to catch, but trout that large are not unusual here.

Fool's Hollow Lake

Fool's Hollow Lake is built atop a field of lava caves. In the past, when a particularly wet season filled the lake, the additional pressure would crack the roof of one of the caves and drain the lake. The latest such breach was plugged in 1984, and the lake is back in business. The 140-acre body of water is on the outskirts of Show Low and offers a mixed bag of largemouth bass, catfish, walleye, and brown trout. The only facility is a small boat launch area.

Luna Lake

Luna Lake manages to keep both Arizona anglers and New Mexico farmers happy. Its seventy-five acres are just a mile or two from the New Mexico line east of Alpine, and water from the lake irrigates land in that state. The lake also is the home of lots of rainbow and brook trout. The weed harvester has helped here too, and the past few years have been some of the best in the lake's history. Luna offers outstanding fly fishing—a favorite with trollers, since outboards to eight horsepower are permitted. The lake has a launch facility, parking, shore fishing, a small store and boat rentals, and an excellent campground.

Lyman Lake

Lyman Lake is where White Mountain water skiers congregate because it's big enough (1400 acres) and warm enough (6000-foot elevation). Lyman has channel catfish, walleye, crappie, yellow perch, northern pike, and largemouth bass, so it's a piscatorial grab bag. Fishing is best from June to October. You'll find a good launch ramp (no motor restrictions) and a small store and boat rental operation, plus an excellent state park campground and swimming beach.

Nelson Reservoir

Nelson Reservoir is popular with the "bait from shore" crowd. It's right beside paved U. S. Route 666 south of Springerville, so access is no problem. Its sixty acres give up brook and brown trout early and late in the year. Rainbows are most prevalent during the summer months. A boat launch, restroom, and a couple of picnic areas are available. Though most fish are pan-size, a few monsters come from Nelson every year, and the knowledge they're there adds spice to any visit.

Fishing

Rainbow Lake

Rainbow Lake is in beautiful Lakeside and has eighty acres of open water. Best fished from a boat, Rainbow has trout of the same name, plus a few big browns that are tougher to catch, and, especially in the spring, some outsize large-mouth bass. There are also legions of bait-stealing sunfish. The shoreline is all private land. Look for a small tract belonging to the Game and Fish Department; it is on the western end of the dam and offers parking and a place to launch a boat. A Forest Service campground is just east of the dam. Motors to eight horsepower are permitted. (The weed harvester has made a big difference here, too.)

Scotts Reservoir

Scotts Reservoir measures eighty acres when full but may shrink to pond-size during dry spells. It's just north of Lakeside and contains rainbow, brown, and brook trout, plus channel catfish and largemouth bass. There are no facilities, and car-top boats are about all you can get on the lake (electrics are the only motors permitted). Since the water gets a bit warm during the summer months, trout fisher-men do best in early spring.

Show Low Lake

Show Low Lake is about halfway between Show Low and Lakeside, and it's another mixed-bag lake. You might catch rainbow or brown trout, catfish (including chunky, good-tasting bullheads), largemouth bass or walleye, and even an occasional northern pike. Winter and early spring are best for trout, although rainbows are stocked during the sum-mer. The lake has a launch ramp, a small store, boat rentals, and a Navajo County Parks camping facility.

Sierra Blanca Lake

Sierra Blanca Lake is small (five acres) and weedy, and it freezes nearly solid each winter, so there's seldom any carry-over of fish. It's stocked with rainbows each spring, and, because the weeds are trout cafeterias, the fish grow quickly. By late summer or early fall, they are chunky twelve- to thirteen-inch bundles of dynamite. It's worth the walk in the last quarter-mile, from Forest Road 249 between Alpine and Big Lake, for some good fly fishing.

White Mountain Streams

You can jump across most White Mountain trout streams, so you won't find the huge calendar-picture rivers some other Western states offer. Most streams wind through dense forests, however, and if you hike a few hundred yards, they offer gorgeous solitude to go with the wild trout. Stretches near campgrounds and resorts are stocked weekly during the busy summer months. The more remote streams have small, wild trout.

East and West Forks of the Black River meet just below Buffalo Crossing, approximately ten miles south of Big Lake on Forest Road 24. The East Fork offers mostly "put-and-take" trout fishing (the hatchery trucks put them in, anglers take them out), as the stream flows beside the road from Buffalo Crossing to Diamond Rock. The West Fork from Thompson Ranch to the campground just above PS Ranch is small, brushy, and hard to fish. Brown trout appear upstream to the Indian reservation boundary, and stocked rainbows are near the campground.

Black River is a good place to get away from the crowd, with about eleven miles of stream to Wildcat Bridge, and then another four to the reservation border. It is mostly for hikers who are interested in small rainbows and an occasional brown trout.

Campbell Blue, Grant, and KP creeks are very small streams that flow into the Blue River south of Alpine and east of U. S. Route 666. They raise wild rainbow trout that seldom are larger than six or seven inches. The area is mostly for backpackers and wilderness lovers.

Silver Creek, about ten miles north of Show Low, repre-sents only about a mile of public water, just below the Silver Creek Hatchery. Rainbows are stocked in the spring, but it's normally too warm during the summer months.

East Fork, Little Colorado River is a very small stream, flowing six miles from Coulter Reservoir to Greer, where it meets the West Fork of the Little Colorado. It sports brook trout and some rainbows.

West Fork, Little Colorado River is another tiny stream. This one begins on the slopes of Mount Baldy, runs under the bridge on State Route 273 at Sheep Crossing, then plunges into wild country on its way to Greer. There are rainbows at the crossing, brookies upstream, and some browns down-stream. Enjoy West Fork's beauty, but don't expect to catch many fish.

Little Colorado River has a bit more water after the various forks join at Greer but is still small. It's stocked weekly during the summer at several locations in the Greer area, mostly with rainbows in the eight- to nine-inch class. There are also some brown trout, especially in the stretch from South Fork junction downstream toward Eagar.

Hunting the White Mountains

Hunters love the White Mountains for their diversity. The pine-spruce-fir forests harbor deer, elk, turkey, bear, and lion, plus a rich mixture of small game. As the land slopes off to the north into lower elevations, junipers appear and then rolling grassland, home of antelope herds.

Below the Mogollon Rim, south of Alpine and Hannagan Meadow, is the rugged country of the Blue River, a wild jumble of peaks and canyons, of mixed juniper and pine, and chaparral thickets that resist all entrance. U. S. Route 666 curves its way through the landscape. Few side roads penetrate the wilderness beyond.

Game management Units 1, 2A, 2B, 2C, 3A (not within map area, northwest of Unit 3B), 3B, and 27 make up the White Mountain area. They serve to delineate the hunting units established by the Arizona Game and Fish Department for people control. Nearly all big-game hunting is by permit, and a hunter must generally choose one of these units — or a combination of several — and confine hunting to them.

Game animals don't recognize these arbitrary boundaries, and there's a good deal of seasonal migration. The antelope in Unit 1, for example, may move back and forth from there to 2C or 2B. Deer and elk may do the same, complicating things a bit by also drifting on and off the Fort Apache Indian Reservation.

There may be some of this movement at almost any time of year, but generally, the deer, elk, and turkey stay in the high country during the summer and fall, drift off into lower elevations for the winter, then gradually follow the snow line back up the mountains in the spring.

Of the ten species of big-game animals found in Arizona, only the buffalo is not found in the White Mountains. Recent plants of Rocky Mountain bighorns have been made to supplement sheep from New Mexico that have drifted into the area, and the Blue Primitive Area seems to be a natural for them. With good natural reproduction and additional plants from other Western states, limited permit hunts will probably continue.

Deer Hunting

Statewide deer-hunting success figures hover around twenty-eight to thirty percent, and most White Mountain areas are average or slightly below. **Mule** and **whitetail** deer are prevalent. Hunts in recent years specify "any antlered deer," and hunters may shoot either species in Unit 27.

The whitetails here are Coues deer. The White Mountain animals have larger bodies and larger antlers but are still part of the same species found mainly in the desert mountains of the southeastern part of the state. Very few white-tails are taken in Unit 1; most come from the country under the Rim in Unit 27.

In years past, a December hunt for whitetails has been held. Because few hunters participated, the unit now has a stratified hunt: early- and late-October seasons and a later hunt during the first half of November. Both are for any antlered deer. Unit 27 is a long way from population centers (as are other White Mountain areas) and has a reputation for rugged terrain, so its drawing odds are good.

Unit 1 is mostly high country, although there are junipers and grassland in the eastern part of the unit, with some mixed pine and juniper south of U.S. Highway 60 from Springerville to Vernon. Years with abundant moisture often trigger a mini-boom in mule deer populations in the spruce-fir-pine areas of this unit, and harvest figures are close to the statewide average.

The hunt opens on the traditional late October Friday and runs to mid-November. Early snows may move the deer off the summer high-elevation ranges into lower country. Preseason scouting just before the hunt is important, and weather can make a marked difference in where you will find deer. If you're new to the area, the country from Alpine to Big Lake, south to the Mogollon Rim, and west to the Indian reservation is a good place to begin.

Unit 2 deer populations are down a bit from previous years, and permit numbers are lower. Few hunters participate, and they are generally locals who know which scattered junipers in which tiny draw might shelter a mule deer buck. Some big deer are taken here, however, and the northern part of the unit is best.

Unit 3 covers mostly juniper-grassland, with some tall pines along the Mogollon Rim from Pinetop to Heber. Success is much higher in the southern half of the unit, since the area north of Snowflake is mostly open grassland. There are some big bucks in the junipers, but hunting is tough, with heavy cover and lower deer numbers than in the pines and mixed juniper-pine areas.

Overall success figures for the White Mountain deer units are probably pushed upward a couple of percentage points by local hunters. They make up the bulk of the permit holders, know the country well, do more scouting, and tend to hunt longer and harder.

Elk Hunting

The White Mountain elk herd is approaching the carrying capacity of the range, so each year's hunt is designed to keep the population numbers within certain limits. The elk herds are in good shape statewide, and more than 2000 animals have been harvested in this region during each of the recent years.

There are firearms, muzzleloaders, and archery hunts in White Mountain units, and seasons stretch from mid-September to late November. The archery season is first, with permit holders hunting in most White Mountain units. The archers are afield during the rut, when bulls are rounding up harems of cows and the woods echo with the high, shrill challenge of the males, making them a bit easier to locate. In spite of the range and accuracy limitations of their weapons, the bow hunters have a ten to twelve percent success rate.

Some White Mountain units may be included in the early hunt for mature bulls (four points or better) and muzzle-loader hunts in the early season are also authorized in selected units some years. Elk management specialists use a number of hunt options to furnish diversity for the hunters while also accomplishing their management objectives.

Many trophy elk hunters consider the late hunt the ultimate challenge. The late November season occasionally includes a few days in early December and hunters can count on snow and very cold temperatures. The elk have often moved out of the high country by this time and the lower juniper or mixed juniper-pine country is the favorite with late season hunters.

Odds on getting drawn for elk continue to widen. Some early hunts in this region have ten to one odds against getting one of the permits. Later hunts are not so bad.

Mule deer

Hunting

Antelope Hunting

Although antelope are fairly easy to see in the White Mountain area, especially along the road from Greer to Eagar and from Springerville to Show Low or St. Johns, overall numbers are limited by available habitat. Total permits for the archery, muzzleloader, and firearms hunts number only 140 or so each year. Success is high for firearms, about seventy to seventy-five percent statewide, but is less than ten percent for archers.

A big part of antelope hunting is getting drawn for a permit, because applications outnumber available permits by five to one in the least-popular areas to more than ten to one in the most-popular units in the White Mountains.

Antelope are highly visible animals and frequently feed close to major highways. Game and Fish enforcement specialists in the White Mountains estimate as many antelope are taken illegally each year as are harvested by permit-holding hunters.

Turkey Hunting

The turkey is a New World bird, unknown in Europe until the Spanish arrived in Mexico and Central America in the early 1500s and one of the first ships returning to Spain took along some of the big birds. Most of the new, exotic things introduced to Spain, Italy, or England in those days seemed to come from the East, and somehow the rumor spread that these large, colorful birds had arrived from Turkey. The name has stuck ever since. So the main ingredient of your Thanksgiving meal is a descendant of the same ancestors as are the wild birds you can hunt today in the White Mountains. In fact, the first time most people see a flock of the birds, their first remark is, "Gee, they look just like turkeys."

Ben Franklin favored the majestic turkey as the national emblem of America; he considered the eagle a nasty, thieving bird. But perhaps it's best that Ben was overruled; it's difficult to imagine a dollar bill with a picture of a turkey on the back.

The forested areas of the White Mountains offer fall turkey hunting that has a success rate about average for the state — ten to fifteen percent. Units 1 and 27 are best, and during the October season the birds are still in the high country. The big birds often feed and water early and late in the day along small streams in the area. There is no permit system in effect for the fall hunt; a hunting license and a turkey tag are all that you need.

Archery deer hunters, afield in late August-early September, may also take turkeys with a bow if they have the proper tag. Archery elk hunters may do the same during their September season.

One of the most challenging big-game hunts in the state is the spring turkey season. It is limited to bearded birds only — usually gobblers — who are mating during the April-May season and can thus be challenged with an artificial call. Unit 1 was the scene of the first such hunt in Arizona in the mid-1960s, and Units 1 and 27 remain the best places to get your Thanksgiving turkey a few months early. Drawing odds on these two popular units are always higher than in other White Mountain units.

Bear Hunting

Because of its rough, broken country, Unit 27 is one of the better spots for bear in the state. Units 1 and 3B also have decent populations. About 200 to 350 bears per year are taken in Arizona, and these three units account for about seventy-five. Most are taken during the fall months, and September and October are the best. Some bears are taken incidental to deer, turkey, or elk hunts. Many hunters buy a bear tag each year — just in case.

Lion Hunting

Statistics and estimates of biologists agree that Arizona mountain lion populations are more or less stable. Even so, it's easy to spend a lifetime hunting in our state and never see a lion. A few are taken each year by hunters looking for other species, but even among those who hunt specifically for lion, the success ratio is low. Most are taken by guides with dogs. The months from October to March are best. Of a possible 200-250 lions taken each year, the White Mountain units account for less than ten percent. The season is open all year long.

Javelina Hunting

Most of the White Mountains are too high for javelina, but the lower portion of Unit 27 does have a population, and a few permits are issued there each year for the March hunting season.

Bighorn Sheep Hunting

The first bighorn sheep hunt in recent times took place in Unit 27 in December 1984. One permit was authorized for a Rocky Mountain bighorn sheep, the first for that species in Arizona history. The majority of the bighorns are found along the San Francisco River in the southern part of Unit 27. They drift back and forth across the Arizona-New Mexico border, but they appear to be present in good enough numbers so a limited permit hunt will take place each year.

Small-Game Hunting

Abert squirrels are found in ponderosa pine stands all across the Rim country, and they are a popular game animal during the October season. **Red squirrels**, somewhat smaller, are found at higher elevations, but most of the effort is expended for Aberts. Look for open, park-like stands of ponderosa.

Hunt **blue grouse** in the higher elevations, above 8500 feet. This chicken-size bird (about two pounds) lives in high country meadows and roosts in nearby trees. Overgrown logging roads are a good bet as well. The feathers are dusky blue and the tail has a band of light-tipped feathers. Mount Baldy, Escudilla Mountain, and the Hannagan area are good places to hunt. The season runs from early September to mid-November with a three-bird daily limit.

Acorns are a favorite food of **bandtail pigeons** in the fall, so look for these birds in oak trees, especially those around waterholes or small lakes. They also relish piñon nuts, berries and, if they can find them, grain crops. Bandtails are federally managed, since they migrate and occasionally fly south before the October season begins. Check the areas just under the Rim and along the Blue River in Unit 27, and anywhere along the band of oaks that marks where the high country begins to slope toward the juniper-grassland.

There are some fairly good **mourning dove** flights in the White Mountains. Anywhere you can find stubble fields, you'll find doves during the September season. The farming belt along Silver Creek in the Snowflake-Taylor area is a good place to begin. But don't expect huge flights like those in the Phoenix and Tucson areas.

The lakes and ponds of the White Mountains raise some **ducks,** mostly mallards and teal, and there's even a couple of small resident flocks of **Canada geese.** Waterfowl hunting is best when the October opening coincides with the early migration of pintail ducks. Many of the so-called lakes shown on White Mountain maps are really shallow, weedy areas that can hold good numbers of ducks. The area south and west of Springerville has a good many of these duck factories. There's some jump shooting along the Little Colorado, downstream from Springerville. Lyman Lake, which seldom freezes, holds some ducks and geese throughout the season. Most of the high country ponds freeze late in November, and except for some isolated areas with open water, that ends the shooting season.

Blue grouse

The Fort Apache Reservation

Nearly 10,000 Native Americans live on the Fort Apache Indian Reservation's 1,664,000 acres in the White Mountains. The tribe's cattle operation raises prize Herefords, and its timber company is the largest employer on the reservation. But the industry for which the White Mountain Apache are most widely known is recreation.

More than two decades ago, the tribe realized the potential their beautifully timbered homeland held as a vacation paradise, and they began actively to welcome visitors from all over the country. And today, if you like to fish, hunt, camp, or just explore the outdoors, the tribe's hope is that you will be a guest.

There are fees, of course, but Apache camping fees are generally less than those charged for campgrounds in the national forests that surround them. And although Apache lakes and streams are heavily stocked from two hatcheries on the reservation, they are not as heavily fished. So the daily fishing fees are a good bargain. Hunting is a bit more expensive. Several of the trophy-type hunts are beyond the economic range of the average outdoorsman. Nevertheless, tribal lands do provide some outstanding trophies, and it's hard to argue with the principle of getting the most out of available resources.

Unlike the situation in the early days of the recreation program, today's tribal game and fish department is completely professional. The director, the wildlife and fisheries biologists, the fully trained and equipped game wardens all are Apache. And every permit bought helps ensure the future of their effort. You are a vital part of the program that benefits tribe and visitor alike.

There are a number of remote areas on the reservation closed to all entry. These are mostly on the slopes of Mount Baldy and Mount Ord. They contain the tiny streams that are the historic home of the Apache trout, *Salmo apache*, a colorful fish found only in Arizona. The Apache have instituted a system whereby some of the wilder stretches of back country have quotas. Only a very limited number of visitors are allowed in these areas at any one time, thus assuring you of a satisfying outdoor experience. Special-use permits to visit these quota areas cost a bit more than a regular Apache camping or fishing license, but considering the quality of the experience, the fees are extremely reasonable.

Summer is the most popular season here. But even then, there are never as many people on Apache lakes or campgrounds as there are in other White Mountain areas. And if even *one* other angler is too many for you, it's easy to choose a stream and walk away from all signs of civilization.

Wise anglers concentrate on spring and fall months, when lake waters are colder and trout more eager. If your timing is just right in the fall and you reach the high lakes before they begin to ice over, it's possible you'll have an entire lake to yourself.

The Fort Apache reservation is a family place. If Dad can find a super camp spot and arrange for Mom and the kids to catch fish, he'll be a hero—at least until the next outing. The Apache understand this feeling and do their best to make it come true.

Although the high country that slopes west and north from 11,590-foot Mount Baldy contains the most lakes and campgrounds and is the most popular, there remains a vast chunk of reservation on the west side. That area is bounded, essentially, by U.S. Route 60 as it winds from the bottom of the Salt River Canyon to Show Low, and it stretches west beyond Sombrero Peak and north to the Mogollon Rim. There are hundreds of thousands of acres of pine, juniper, and grasslands visited by only an occasional cowboy. The only community is Cibecue, and the few visitors who come to this area mostly camp and fish along Cibecue Creek.

Delightfully, for campers, fishermen, and hunters, the Fort Apache Indian Reservation is huge, lightly touched by the hand of man, sparsely populated, and, for most of the year, more reflective of the Old West than the New West.

(Above left) A good hunter and his binoculars are inseparable. Rick Odell

(Right) The Fort Apache Indian Reservation is one of the top black bear spots in Arizona. The Apache complain of "too many bear," and a hunter who can afford the permit and guide fees is pretty well assured of a rug in his den. Judd Cooney

(Above) Apache country is remote and rugged, just the sort that lions prefer. Judd Cooney

(Left) There are wild places on the Fort Apache reservation where man does not set foot from year to year. Jerry Jacka

(Below) The White Mountain Apache Tribe offers the state's top hunt for trophy bull elk, but permits are expensive. Judd Cooney

(Left) Hawley Lake was one of the first Apache lakes built for recreation, and it remains a high, cool favorite. Jerry Jacka

(Right) At its best, fishing is a contemplative sport. Gill Kenny

(Below) Rainbows this big fall into the lunker class. Judd Cooney

(Bottom) It's not far from the lake to the frying pan at Shush Be Tou Lake. Dick Dietrich

(Following panel, pages 110-111) The White River winds through some of the best of Apache country. It is stocked often during the summer months in the most accessible sections. The remaining miles appeal to backpackers who also like to fish. David Muench

(Left to right) Mallard. Judd Cooney
Green-winged teal. Thomas Danielsen
Canada goose. James Tallon

Horseshoe Cienega Lake claims the record brown trout—
over sixteen pounds. Its rich waters hold rainbow and
brook trout as well. Gill Kenny

(Following panel, pages 114-115) Virtually every wet spot in the state has mallards in season...along with pintails, widgeons, teal, scaup, redheads, canvasbacks, buffleheads, gadwalls, and goldeneyes. Larry Toschik.

(Above) Apache country is remote and rugged, just the sort that lions prefer. Judd Cooney

(Left) There are wild places on the Fort Apache reservation where man does not set foot from year to year. Jerry Jacka

(Below) The White Mountain Apache Tribe offers the state's top hunt for trophy bull elk, but permits are expensive. Judd Cooney

Region 6

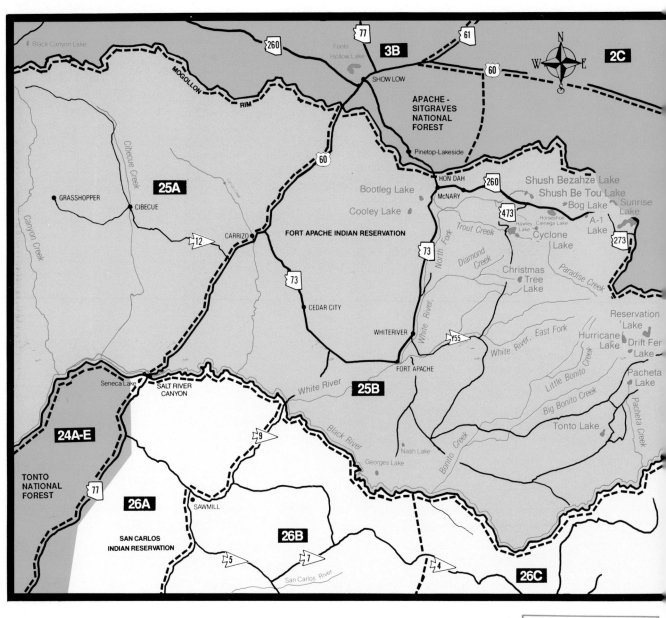

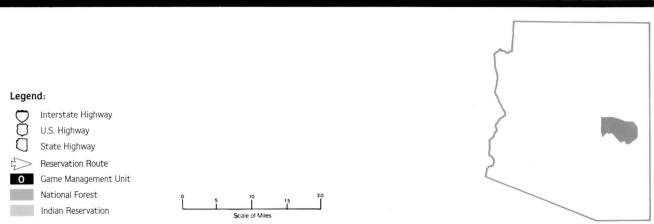

Legend:

- Interstate Highway
- U.S. Highway
- State Highway
- Reservation Route
- **0** Game Management Unit
- National Forest
- Indian Reservation

Scale of Miles
0   5   10   15   20

Fishing the Fort Apache Reservation

If you like to catch trout, this is the place to be. The Apaches have more than 400 miles of streams and about two dozen lakes, most of which are stocked with trout. This is the home of the Arizona native trout, *Salmo apache*, but rainbow, brook, brown, and cutthroat trout are what most anglers put in the frying pan.

The fish come from two federal hatcheries, at Williams Creek and Alchesay, but no trout from the Arizona Game and Fish Department hatcheries are stocked on the reservation. Daily fishing fees tend to keep the lakes and streams uncrowded.

And now that the U.S. Supreme Court has ruled that Indians do indeed have sole jurisdiction over the fish and wildlife on their lands, it's possible to catch two limits of trout in one day. With an Apache permit, you could take one from Reservation Lake in the morning, then drive nine miles to Big Lake, on national forest land off the Apache reservation, and take another limit with an Arizona state fishing license — and be perfectly legal.

A few Apache trout lakes have stores, boat rental docks, and even cabins, but most are pristine, with only a campground tucked back in the pines. Like most other high-country trout waters, Apache lakes and streams are best early and late in the year, even though most of the action occurs during the summer months.

White Mountain Apache Lakes

Tonto Lake was opened to the public (that is, non-tribal members) in 1948. This remote, eighty-acre lake has had an up-and-down career because of a leak in the lake bottom that has caused the lake to disappear several times over the years. It's been fixed, and some new special regulations have been imposed. Non-tribal members may fish only on Friday, Saturday, and Sunday, and the daily fee is a bit higher than the normal Apache permit cost.

The Indians are managing the lake to produce large trout, so besides the abundant pan-size fish, there's always an excellent chance to catch a trout of fifteen to twenty inches. Access is over narrow, dusty back roads, but the potential rewards are worth the extra effort.

A-1 Lake is right beside paved State Route 260, so you can almost fish out the car window. It is popular year round and usually has safe ice during the winter. The catch is mostly pan-size rainbow trout, but anglers have a chance at larger brook trout using flies in the shallow, weedy upper end of the lake, especially late in the day during summer and fall months. Most fish are taken on bait, fished from shore near the dam or parking area. A-1 is just twenty-four acres, but a super producer.

Shush Bezahze Lake is better known as **Little Bear** which is much easier to pronounce than the Apache name. It is just off State Route 260 east of Pinetop, and this small (fifteen-acre) lake puts out lots of pan-size rainbows.

There's a chance at big brown trout as snow and ice disappear in early spring. Popular with the "bait from shore" group, Little Bear nevertheless is seldom crowded. There is a small, casual campground.

Shush Be Tou Lake is also known as **Big Bear**. It is an eighteen-acre lake just upstream (Bog Creek) from its smaller neighbor. Conditions are similar to those of its little brother, and the same seven- to nine-inch rainbows are on tap. A small campground decorates the shoreline.

Bog Tank is the third member of this group. Its twelve acres are near the head of Bog Creek; the Bear lakes are downstream. Bog Tank's earthen dam and small size make the "tank" name suitable, because cattlemen all across the state construct this same kind of water catchment for livestock, and Bog Tank was first constructed for this purpose. It is stocked regularly with pan-size rainbows, with a scattering of brook or brown trout possible, too. Boats are seldom seen because most fishing is from shore. There is good fly fishing on summer afternoons in the shallow, stump-infested upper end of the lake.

Sunrise Lake is large (870 acres when full), immensely productive, and one of the best fish-growing lakes in the state. There are lots of rainbows in the ten- to twelve-inch class, and almost every stringer will include a few fish in the fourteen- to eighteen-inch category. There's always a chance, too, of hooking one of the lake's abundant population of lunker trout — fish from two to five pounds and up. The upper end of the lake is weedy and shallow, but the weedbeds are full of food, so fly fishing is always a good bet. Shore anglers stick to bait, and they concentrate on the north and west sides of the lake, from the dam up to the park/launch area on the north shoreline. A good way for boat fishermen to succeed is to troll with long gangs of spinners, followed by a hook full of worms — the so-called Ford Fender rigs.

The Sunrise Hotel is on the shore of the lake, with nice rooms and good food. During the summer season, a store offers fishing tackle, bait and camper type groceries. They also rent boats, with or without motors. Outboards to eight horsepower are allowed on Sunrise, the only reservation lake where they are permitted. Ice fishing is popular here in the January-March period. There's a free launch ramp (don't forget a tribal boat permit) on the north shore, another at the upper end of the lake near the cinder pit.

Bootleg Lake is just a couple of miles south of Hon Dah off State Route 73, and this ten-acre pond offers channel catfish and Florida-strain largemouth bass. The access road can be rough. The campground is small and primitive.

Cooley Lake is better for history buffs than anglers. Corydon E. Cooley, a scout for General George Crook, won the famous card game that caused the naming of a town when he was able to "Show Low." Cooley had a homestead near the lake that bears his name. The eleven-acre pond is just south of Hon Dah off State Route 73 and contains

Fishing

channel catfish and some Florida-strain largemouth bass. There are half a dozen sites in the campground here.

Reservation Lake offers an opportunity to catch at least a few trout on every visit. This 280-acre lake is set in a thick spruce-fir forest and offers an opportunity at a stringer that includes rainbow, brook, and brown trout. Although most fish are pan-size, there's an excellent chance at landing one in the twelve- to sixteen-inch class. A store offers permits, groceries, and rental boats from May to September, and there's a campground on a ridge overlooking the lake. Shore fishing is okay almost anywhere on the lake, trollers do well from boats, and there is usually good fly fishing late in the afternoons during the late summer-early fall months. It's seldom crowded and always good for some fish.

Christmas Tree Lake is at the junction of Sun and Moon creeks and it is one of the loveliest spots in the state. The fish it holds—Arizona native trout—are lovely too.

Salmo apache and another small native trout, *Salmo gila*, were the only game fish found in the state when Europeans arrived. The small, high streams of the Fort Apache reservation are the historic habitat of the Apache trout. They are found nowhere else in the world. Christmas Tree Lake holds pure specimens that are part of the Apache management plan to insure the trout's survival. The lake is open to fishing during the summer months with a minimum number of anglers allowed each day, a fee befitting the experience, a sharply reduced limit, and the use of single barbless hook flies or lures only. But you can catch a slice of history.

Pacheta Lake is a bit off the beaten track in the thick woods south of Reservation Lake. The unpaved roads and lack of fancy facilities are discouraging to some, but most fishermen appreciate the solitude and the chance at rainbow and brown trout. The browns, especially, tend to get big enough to get your picture in the paper when you land one. The campground has twenty-five very casual sites.

Cyclone Lake is a few miles northeast of Hawley Lake at 8100 feet elevation. The thirty-seven acre bit of paradise is open only by special arrangement. The Apaches call it "rent a lake." You pay a fee (plus so much for each person) for you and your group—church, fellow employees, civic club, family reunion, school, etc.—and you have the lake all to yourselves. Camp, fish, party, or whatever. Lots of trout in the lake, including some big ones. Cool, quiet and peaceful — at least till your gang arrives! Check with the Apache Game and Fish office for details.

Hurricane Lake was renovated and stocked with native trout (Salmo apache) a few years ago but it turned out some rainbows remained. Now the two species have hybridized. There's a summer season, a special fee and you may keep only one native trout. But the Apaches encourage you to catch and keep the rainbows and hybrids. Many of the fish are in the fourteen to sixteen inch class. Use single barbless

hook flies and lures only. The lake is just off the road between Reservation Lake and Drift Fence Lake.

Drift Fence Lake is about sixteen acres of shallow water set in a meadow surrounded by aspen and spruce-fir forest. It's so gorgeous in the fall that it's hard to keep your mind on the rainbow and brook trout. Because it is shallow, Drift Fence usually loses its fish during the winter freeze; but fresh stocks are planted when the road opens in the spring and again in midsummer, and most are taken out by anglers. The rich water puts inches and pounds on trout quickly, and there are twelve- to fourteen-inch fish by the fall months. Abundant underwater insect life means good fly fishing. A small campground serves anglers.

Horseshoe Cienega Lake is set in a big horseshoe-shaped meadow. Weed beds provide lots of trout food, and fly fishing is especially good in the shallow upper end of the 120-acre lake. Shore anglers stick with bait and favor the shoreline on the dam and near the campground, which is one of the largest and best on the reservation. There are rainbow, brook, and brown trout here, and taking all three species in one day is not unusual. Most are in the eight- to ten-inch class, but lunkers to sixteen pounds have been taken here. There is good ice fishing, with access off State Route 260 about eighteen miles east of Pinetop. A small store and boat-rental dock are open from May to September.

Earl Park Lake is overshadowed by nearby Hawley Lake, but its forty-seven acres nevertheless offer cutthroat and brook trout. There are lots of weeds, so a boat is a big help; fly fishing is productive.

Hawley Lake has become familiar on TV weather reports as the coldest spot in the state. Hawley's 260 acres kicked off the tribe's lake-building program during the late 1950s and 1960s. There are mostly rainbows here, with cutthroat, brook, and brown trout possible; some big browns are taken through the ice. Hawley offers a large campground, store, rental boats, and permits all year. The access road is paved.

Warm water tanks: The Apache have stocked a number of small cattle watering tanks or ponds with channel catfish. Most of these tanks are on Bonito Prairie, south of old Fort Apache. Some of the larger impoundments may also contain bass or bluegills. The Apache game and fish office in Whiteriver can tell you which ponds are best.

White Mountain Apache Streams

The Apache stock the most popular streams several times each month during the busy summer season. Rainbow trout in the eight- to nine-inch class are planted in a number of locations along the northern and eastern forks of the White River, and in Diamond Creek, Paradise Creek, and Cibecue Creek. Other, smaller creeks are not stocked, but do contain wild trout that have drifted out of lakes or other streams and reproduced.

North Fork, White River is a super stream that runs for

miles as the main water source on the northern part of the reservation from Sunrise Lake to the town of Whiteriver. Its flow roughly parallels State Route 260 from A-1 Lake to Hon Dah and State Route 73 from there to Fort Apache. Heavily stocked and heavily fished at road crossings and campgrounds, the North Fork offers some solitude to those who don't mind walking. There are rainbows, with some browns in more remote sections, and occasional brookies or cutthroats. It is generally too warm for trout in the section below Whiteriver.

East Fork, White River has mostly rainbow trout on a put-and-take basis, but some good browns inhabit the deeper pools. Easy access is provided via Apache Route Y-55, and that means lots of competition. Upper reaches are closed. They contain protected native trout.

Diamond Creek is open only during the summer months. A special permit is needed and regulations allow one trout over sixteen inches and five trout eight inches or less, plus the use of single barbless hook flies and lures only. Mostly brown trout in this small, brushy, hard to fish stream along Apache Road R-25.

Cibecue Creek is stocked with rainbows in the stretch above the town of Cibecue, on the western side of the reservation. There are some good browns in remote pools.

Paradise Creek is open only for a mile above its junction with the North Fork of the White River. It is stocked, but the fish are small and the going is tough.

Bonito Creek is a special permit area, accessible only to backpackers. It offers wild trout in wild surroundings.

Black River consists of about sixty miles of smallmouth-bass water in some of the wildest country in the state. A few four-wheel-drive roads touch the stream, and there's a bridge at Black River Crossing, a few miles upstream from the junction of the Black and the White. Otherwise, you must backpack. Your reward is superb fishing; many fishermen take fifty smallmouths a day and up. It is very rough walking, with constant wading back and forth across the river. The threat of tangling with a bear or rattlesnake makes this river suitable only for those who are in good physical condition and who are fully aware of the challenges. The Black River is the southern boundary of the Fort Apache reservation; the San Carlos Apache Tribe is on the south bank. A special permit is required, so check with Apache game and fish officials in Whiteriver.

Other streams: Reservation, Pacheta, Trout, Canyon, and the upper Black River all have trout but are not regularly stocked. For walkers only, the area is lonesome and unspoiled. Some stretches of these streams won't see an angler from one year to the next.

Some anglers brave chilly early spring weather at Hawley Lake in hopes of landing a lunker rainbow or brown. Dick Dietrich

Hunting the Fort Apache Reservation

Because the Fort Apache reservation is private land, owned and administered by the White Mountain Apache Tribe, hunting regulations and fees have always been different from those of the state and federal land outside the reservation in Arizona. This difference has increased in the past decade, especially in the case of big game hunts.

The average hunter can still pursue the abundant small game on the reservation, and the javelina permit is not too expensive. But pursuit of elk, bear, lion, or antelope has become the elite sport of trophy hunters who can afford to pay high fees for the opportunity to take an animal that may make one or more of the big-game record books.

Arizona regulations strictly limit the amount of game a hunter may take, and those limits formerly applied to the reservation as well. But a 1983 U.S. Supreme Court decision changed all that. The court decided that Indian tribes have exclusive jurisdiction over the wildlife of their reservations.

This means that if a hunter is properly licensed by the White Mountain Apache, he may take a bear, elk, lion, or other big game animal for which the tribe has an open season. Game taken on the reservation has no effect on what a hunter may take elsewhere.

This rule also applies to a limit of quail, squirrels, blue grouse, or other legal game, big or small.

Certain parts of the reservation are closed to hunting and/or entry, and fees, regulations, and seasons may change without notice. Check with the tribal game and fish office in Whiteriver before you go afield.

Elk Hunting

A limited number of permits is authorized each fall (September-October) for trophy bull elk, with permits in the eight to twelve thousand dollar range. The fee includes a fully guided hunt and usually a chance at a very large elk. These hunts are always sold out a year in advance, so contact the Apache well ahead of time if interested.

Bear Hunting

Bear permits are not expensive, but you must have a guide — approved by the Apache — before you hunt, and that can make the excursion more costly. Tribal regulations permit the taking of two bears per year, and the huge reservation is an excellent place to hunt. The Apache have too many bears, and they are a nuisance during the summer months when they raid campground garbage cans for easy meals. The season is open fall, winter, and spring.

Lion Hunting

Lion hunters have the same basic costs as bear hunters: a nominal fee for the permit, a stiffer cost for the mandatory guided hunt. Lion numbers are never high, although studies show sport hunting has little effect on overall populations.

You can expect a tougher, perhaps longer hunt than for bear. The season is year-round. Your hunt will probably take you into the most remote and rugged parts of the reservation.

Antelope Hunting

The tribe's game and fish department biologists authorize permits only for the number of trophy antelope present in the herds each year, often as few as three or four. As in the case of elk, permits cost several thousand dollars. The herd is found on Bonito Prairie, south of Fort Apache.

Javelina Hunting

Permit costs are moderate on the Fort Apache and the three week javelina season is open for archery or firearms hunting. There are a limited number of permits available and they are sold on a first-come basis. With permits increasingly difficult to come by in the state hunt, this is an excellent alternative. Most of the javelina are on the western side of the reservation, along the Salt River or along the western boundary of the reservation between Canyon Creek and the Sierra Ancha. The area is lightly hunted and offers an escape from the crowd.

Deer and Turkey Hunting

There are presently no deer or turkey hunts for non-tribal members.

Small-Game Hunting

This may be the reservation's biggest bargain. For one fee, a hunter may pursue rabbits, dove, quail, squirrel, grouse, bandtail pigeon, and waterfowl, usually without a lot of competition from other hunters.

Excellent concentrations of **bandtails** — probably the best in the state — occur along both forks of the White River and on the western side of the reservation in the Cibecue area, and the patient hunter with a good dog usually can locate **blue grouse** on McKay's Peak.

The White and Black rivers combine just below old Fort Apache to form the Salt River, and all three streams raise some **ducks** each summer, mostly mallards and teal. They also serve as resting places for migrating ducks, and even after ponds in other areas of the White Mountains are frozen, the rivers furnish open water and concentrations of waterfowl, both ducks and **geese**. The Salt River, especially in the remote reaches downstream from the Black River-White River junction, is lightly hunted and always holds birds. Just getting close enough to the river to hike in is difficult, and sneaking the river banks, hoping to push a flock of gaudy mallards into the air, is further hard work. But chances are you'll not be bothered by other hunters, and finding at least some ducks or geese is fairly well assured. Most waterfowlers simply won't work this hard.

The reservation has huge stands of ponderosa pine, including the parklike groves that are the choice of the **Abert tree squirrel**, and almost nobody bothers to hunt these areas. **Dove** hunting is a minor sport here, but there are some local flights of mourning doves during the early September season.

Quail hunting on the western side of the reservation is very good, with wide areas that are never hunted from year to year. Always a good bet are the desert areas along the Salt River, downstream from the Salt River bridge on U.S. Route 60 to the Tonto National Forest boundary, and the long ridges between Canyon Creek and the reservation's western border. There may be isolated populations of scaled and Mearn's quail, but most of the birds are the familiar top-knotted Gambel's. The number of quail fluctuates with winter-spring rain, just as in other parts of the state.

Elk

Region 7
Central Arizona

There is a certain satisfaction in being able to turn your back on a million people, travel for an hour or two, and find a wild, lonesome spot where time seemingly stands still, and the West is still the way it used to be. The central part of the state has hundreds of thousands of residents, yet nearby, there are hundreds of thousands of acres of rugged wilderness.

You can hunt rabbits on the desert in the morning and catch trout for lunch the same day on Tonto Creek. Or you can spend a sunny January morning on Apache Lake fishing for bass, then put the boat on the beach, walk up a brush-lined wash, and collect a brace or two of quail. And somewhere in this huge region there is a perfect place to camp every month of the year, and you can choose the shade of a saguaro or a pine, depending on the season.

The two-hour drive from the Phoenix area to the base of the Mogollon Rim, north of Payson, is a vivid lesson in the difference between life zones. The land gradually changes from a creosote and paloverde desert to a high desert landscape of jojoba and mesquite, then to juniper and agave and finally to oak and pine. You've traveled a hundred miles or so, climbed nearly a mile in elevation, and seen the difference a few hundred feet can make in rainfall patterns, ground cover, plant communities, and the kinds of birds and animals that live in a particular area.

The desert has bloomed because man-made dams mean a dependable supply of water. And every year, thousands of anglers go home from the Salt and Verde River reservoirs with sunburns, happy memories, and the ingredients for a fish fry. Water is an irresistible magnet to desert dwellers, so fishermen and campers share the lakes with water skiers and pleasure boaters.

In the Mazatzal Mountains and Sierra Ancha, during the mellow days of autumn, wild turkeys flit through the jack pines while tassel-eared squirrels chatter in branches overhead. In those ranges' lower reaches, it's quail time. The talented Gambel's, almost suited for Olympic running events, lead puffing hunters up and down ridges that slant down from the high peaks.

Trucks from the fish hatcheries have ceased their visits to small streams, but countless hungry trout remain in the deep pools and beneath overhanging banks. Autumn is the time to catch them if you can.

Later in the fall, when the high-country air hints of snows to come and oak leaves crackle and crunch underfoot, the mule deer bucks feed at first light, then slip away to bed in an aspen thicket. The American wapiti, or elk, is legal game in Arizona. And if you're lucky, you may win one of the precious computer-drawn permits that govern the hunt. A mature bull elk is king of the forest, an elusive thousand-pound wraith that drifts through the groves like evaporating mist.

Everywhere, it seems, there are new trails to explore, new lakes to fish, new camping sites to claim, new experiences to share with friends — and new things to learn about yourself.

(Left) Besides offering smallmouth bass, Apache Lake has an excellent population of largemouth bass, catfish, crappie, and panfish. Tony Mandile

(Right) It may be January on the calendar, but it's shirt-sleeve fishing weather on Apache Lake. James Tallon

(Following panel, pages 124-125) Canyon Lake, along the Apache Trail, is home to some outstanding largemouth bass. Many anglers predict the next state record bass will come from here. Jerry Jacka

(Above) A bass from Roosevelt Lake—good eatin' size.
James Tallon

(Right) Roosevelt Dam on the Salt River impounds one of
the best bass lakes in the nation. Nyle Leatham

(Below) Two friends fish for crappie on Roosevelt Lake.
James Tallon

(Bottom) A fisherman launches at Lake Pleasant, northwest of Phoenix. James Tallon

(Top) A duck blind is where a Labrador retriever wants to be. Norm Smith

(Above) Pintails on the wing. They usually arrive early in Arizona's duck season. James Tallon

(Above right) Checking the decoys before the first flight arrives. Norm Smith

(Right) Sunset on Picacho Reservoir, a good spot for ducks, doves, catfish, and bass. Norm Smith

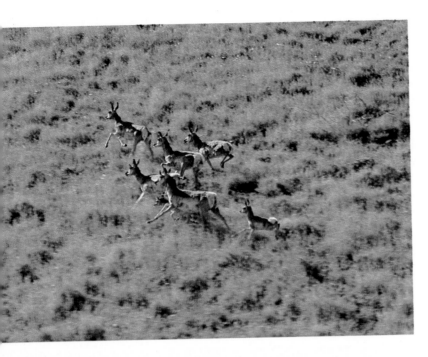

(Far left) A band of antelope north of Phoenix. Jerry Jacka

(Left) The desert grows lots of bobcats, though the secretive creatures are seldom seen. Norm Smith

(Right) A desert mule deer stares at an interloper. Norm Smith

(Below right) A migrating bandtail pigeon pauses on a dead limb. James Tallon

(Below) Opening day of dove season is part social event, part hunt. Studies show hunting has an insignificant effect on dove numbers. James Tallon

(Following panel, pages 132-133) The mountain lion, America's largest wild cat, roams rugged wilderness country throughout most of Arizona. Larry Toschik

A shotgunner and his dog — ready for a day of hunting together. James Tallon

Region 7

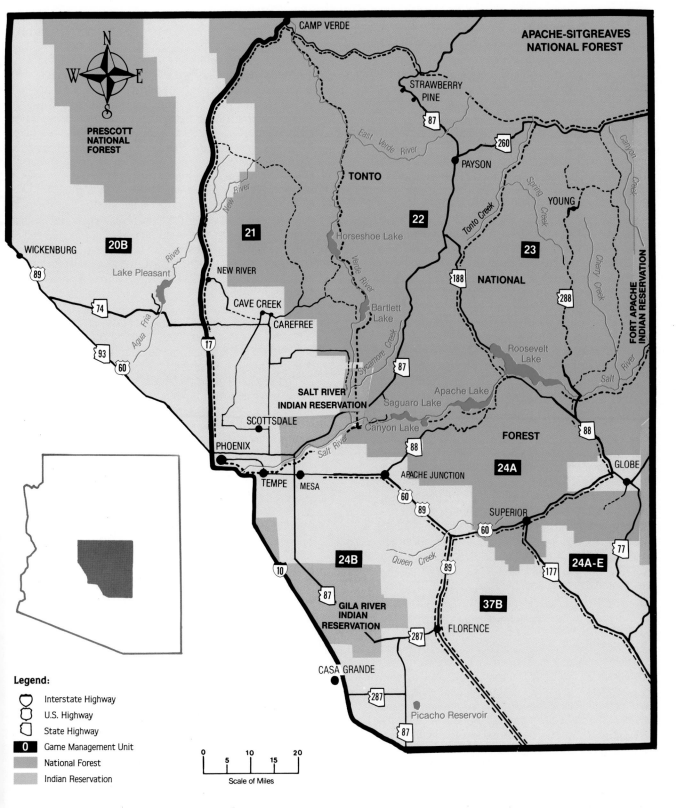

Legend:
- Interstate Highway
- U.S. Highway
- State Highway
- **0** Game Management Unit
- National Forest
- Indian Reservation

0   5   10   15   20
Scale of Miles

Fishing Central Arizona

It was in March 1911 that Teddy Roosevelt led a caravan of open touring cars up the dusty Apache Trail to dedicate and activate the dam that bears his name. The twenty-five or so vehicles in the entourage may have been most of the cars in Arizona at the time. But since the day Teddy pushed the button to drop the gates that filled Roosevelt Lake, millions of other cars and people have visited this giant, historic reservoir.

Roosevelt was joined by Apache, Canyon, and Saguaro lakes on the Salt River, by Bartlett and Horseshoe lakes on the Verde River, and by Lake Pleasant on the Agua Fria. All these reservoirs were built for irrigation and/or power generation but were stocked with fish and quickly became favorites of anglers. Their waters are also a magnet to pleasure boaters and water skiers. Spring and summer weekends tend to be perfect illustrations of how popular water recreation can become in a desert state.

The seven lakes are stocked primarily with such warmwater species as bass, bluegill, crappie, and catfish — with some important exceptions that we'll point out as we discuss the individual lakes. Because of demands for irrigation and municipal water, lake levels can flucuate sharply, as much as forty or fifty vertical feet within a twelve-month period. This yo-yo effect is beneficial to the fish. When the level is down, vegetation grows on the exposed banks. When new water pours in from snowmelt and spring rains, it is full of nutrients. The plants flooded over provide places for young fish to hide, feed, and grow. Good to excellent fishing is the long-term result.

Arizona fishing has no closed season, and anglers can enjoy their sport twenty-four hours a day every day. Because elevations at the desert lakes in this region are all below 2200 feet, the weather is mild enough that fishermen are on the water every month of the year. Techniques differ from season to season, but it's entirely possible to catch a limit of largemouth bass, let's say, on January first, April fifteenth, August fourth, or October tenth. As a result, the lakes in central Arizona get used more than any other waters in the state. And it's a very rare day that they don't yield some fish for the patient angler.

Roosevelt Lake

Roosevelt Lake is the oldest reservoir in the state, and one of the best for fishermen. It has a maximum surface acreage of 17,000, but the level fluctuates from one part of the year to another, depending on runoff from snow melt and rains on the watershed. When you're standing on the dam facing midlake, the Salt River arm of the lake is to the right, or east; the Tonto Creek arm to the left, or northwest.

Roosevelt grows fish fast because it is relatively shallow. It has some brush-filled bays that provide excellent spawning areas, and the water is rich in nutrients from the two inflows. Because it stays warm year-round, fish growth is constant.

Largemouth bass are the main target for most anglers. The state-record bass was caught here: a fourteen-pound, two-ounce monster; but the average fish is one and a half pounds, with a good number at five or six pounds. There are some smallmouth bass as well. They are generally caught on the same kind of lures and in the same places as the more abundant largemouths. Roosevelt also claims the state record for smallmouths, a six-pound, fourteen-ounce dandy.

Bass spawn in the spring when water temperatures reach about sixty-five degrees. Because they're in shallow water then, they're easier to find and catch. April, May, and early June are the best times. Casual anglers most often make their trips during this period, knowing in advance they'll catch some fish and have not-too-hot, not-too-cold weather. Shallow to deep-running plugs, called "crankbaits," are popular in the spring, as are plastic worms, worked slowly along the bottom. Worms can be rigged on "weedless hooks," and the fisherman can toss them into brushy cover with some hope of getting them back.

During summer months you'll find bass foraging in the shallows early and late in the day and retreating to deeper, cooler water the rest of the time. Because of the heat, night fishing is popular during the summer and is a good way to avoid heavy boat traffic from skiers and pleasure craft. Fall months are pleasant for fish and fishermen, and there's a mini-repeat of the good spring action. During the winter, the bass go deep, and anglers need to prospect in water thirty-five to fifty feet deep.

Roosevelt contains channel and flathead catfish. The channel cats are the most abundant, averaging one to three pounds, with occasional catches above ten. The flatheads can reach thirty or forty pounds. Warm spring and summer months are best.

Crappies move into the shallows to spawn in the March-to-May period. There's no limit on the great speckled beauties, and when the bite is "on," hundreds of boats cluster in the hot spots and fishing takes on a circus atmosphere. Roosevelt produces crappies to three pounds, with one-pound fish most common.

There are millions of bluegills and green sunfish in the lake, and although most are too small to bother with, they do delight kids, who can catch as many as they wish with a fishing pole and a can of worms.

There are paved launch ramps on the Tonto and Salt River arms of the lake and another near the dam, where a complete marina is located. Camping is allowed along the lakeshore, but facilities are minimal.

Fishing

Apache Lake

Apache Lake is the second in the chain of four lakes on the Salt River northeast of Phoenix. It's the least-visited because the marina-resort area is smack in the middle of twenty-five miles of narrow, unpaved road. Actually, this section of the Apache Trail, State Route 88, is negotiable with any sort of vehicle, including motorhomes and travel trailers. But the Trail, and especially Fish Creek Hill, have attained such an awesome reputation for being steep and crooked that a good many people are frightened away.

Apache has a steep, rocky shoreline around most of its 2600-acre surface, so although it contains the same species as Roosevelt, plus some important additions, fishing techniques are a bit different. Plastic worms and lures cast close to cliff faces and allowed to sink do very well. So do deep-diving lures worked in deep sections of the shoreline. Apache does have shallow areas, too, and they generally produce bass best in spring and fall.

Besides largemouth bass, catfish, crappie, and panfish, Apache has an excellent population of smallmouth bass. They seem to favor the clear water, cooler temperatures, and rocky shoreline. These qualities make Apache suitable for walleyes, which are stocked yearly. Arizona anglers don't take the big stringers common in eastern parts of the U.S., but late winter-spring months do see some good catches.

Apache also has a sizable number of yellow bass, more popularly known as "stripies." They are school fish, so if you find one, you'll find more. They seldom grow larger than a pound, but they are scrappy fighters on light tackle and are good to eat. They relish minnows, so any small spoon or spinner will work, as do tiny maribou jigs.

Interestingly, Canyon Lake, just downstream from Apache, receives stocks of rainbow trout during the winter months — and when water from Canyon is pumped back up into Apache every day, some of the trout also make the trip. Although there aren't enough rainbows in Apache to fish for them on purpose, every week some bass or crappie fan is surprised to land a trout — often one as large as five or six pounds.

There's a good full-service marina at Apache, with rental boats, launch ramp, cafe, motel, trailer park, and boat storage. They even have houseboats for rent, so you can really rough it while you chase fish. There are two small Forest Service campgrounds.

Canyon Lake

Canyon Lake is well named. The main body of the lake splashes against high cliffs that lead to higher mountains, and the rest of the lake is contained within a steep, winding canyon that weaves through a rugged landscape to the foot of the dam that contains Apache. So, although the surface of Canyon is just 950 acres, it has twenty-eight miles of rocky, mostly up-and-down shoreline. You fish cliffs, submerged boulders, and piles of rock rubble. Bass, catfish, walleye, yellow bass, and sunfish are the main attraction. But because the lake lacks the nutrients and shallow, brushy bays that make Roosevelt such an excellent bass lake, fishing here is tougher. Anglers who prospect with deep-diving lures or plastic worms and jigs do have a chance to land big largemouth bass. Fish over ten pounds come from Canyon every year — but not many.

Water temperatures in Canyon dip to levels that support trout. Each month, from November to March, Game and Fish Department hatchery trucks make visits with loads of rainbow trout in the ten- to twelve-inch class. Most of these fish are caught within weeks, but some survive and from time to time some big trout are taken.

Access is via State Route 88 from Apache Junction, and the highway is paved to the lake. Facilities include a big marina with all services, a Tonto National Forest boat launch ramp, campground, and picnic and swimming areas. Nearby there's a touch of civilization at the tiny community of Tortilla Flat.

Saguaro Lake

Saguaro Lake has the distinction of being the most over-loved lake in the state. Its 1260 acres are surrounded by rugged mountains, so access to the shoreline is extremely limited. So much so, that on summer weekends the parking areas fill up, and there is simply no more room. The lake "closes." There's still ample room on the water — just no place else to put visitors on land.

Because Saguaro is the bottom lake on the four-lake chain, it inherits all the fish species found in the lakes above it. Bass and catfish are the main items on the menu, but anglers can also catch yellow bass, walleye, and an occasional trout, as well as lots of sunfish. All the lakes have more than ample numbers of carp. While these usually hated rough fish can be muddy and unappetitizing if taken from stagnant water, the clear, cold depths of Saguaro and the other Salt River lakes produce carp that taste very good indeed. Would-be gourmets just have to get over the idea that carp are supposed to be inedible.

Saguaro gets an inordinate amount of pleasure-boat traffic, so serious anglers choose very early or late hours of the day, fish at night during the summer, or choose the cooler winter months to avoid competition. Some nice bass and catfish come from Saguaro, but, like Canyon, fishing here is a bit more challenging.

There are two Forest Service launch ramps at Saguaro, plus a ramp, for a fee, at the marina. The marina includes all services as well. Access is via the Bush Highway north of Mesa or off State Route 87 northeast of Fountain Hills.

Fishing

Horseshoe Lake

Horseshoe Lake's fishing can vary from very good to almost nothing at all. The reservoir on the Verde River above Bartlett Lake acts as a water storage lake in wet years. If the water is not completely drained into Bartlett, the bass and crappies spawn and there can be excellent fishing. That happened most recently in the mid to late eighties. Often, however, the lake is little more than a pond behind the big dam, with the Verde flowing through mud flats above it. Since the lake level fluctuates so dramatically, boat launching can be perilous. Tonto National Forest crews do the best they can to keep the launch area usuable but check conditions before you head for Horseshoe.

Bartlett Lake

Bartlett Lake is relatively small (2700 surface acres) but an excellent producer of largemouth bass, crappie, and catfish, especially outsize flathead cats. The waters of the Verde River drain a huge area of central Arizona, and they dump a daily load of nutrients into Bartlett that seem to be just what is needed to produce a rich food chain. It starts with zooplankton, organisms so small the average angler is never aware they exist, and ends up with a fifty-pound flathead catfish or a five-pound bass.

The road to Bartlett, unimproved since the dam was built, is due to be paved late in 1988. Up to now fishermen have been the main users of Bartlett, mostly because the eleven miles of unpaved road discouraged most others. Now that will change. The lake is forty-eight miles from Phoenix via Carefree. It's about 1000 feet higher than the Phoenix area, so conditions are pleasant year round except for the summer months, and even then the nights are moderate.

Fishing is the order of the day on Bartlett. Spring runs of crappie are good to excellent, and spring, summer, and fall bass fishing is always reliable. Along with Roosevelt, most bass fans rate Bartlett as the best place in central Arizona to tangle with a bass. The flathead catfish are recent additions, stocked in the 1970s. Channel catfish abound as well, but it's the monster-type flatheads that get all the attention. It's only a matter of time before some angler wrestles a behemoth from Bartlett that will tip the scales at more than sixty pounds.

Facilities are casual to nonexistent. There is a parking lot/launch area, and Forest Road 459 parallels the lake on the western side for about five miles. There are a number of turnoffs that lead to Rattlesnake Cove, SB Cove, and Bartlett Flat, among other waterside park-and-fish areas.

Verde River

The Verde River offers fair catfishing as it winds through central Arizona. The eastern bank of the river generally is inaccessible, protected by the Mazatzal Wilderness Area; no roads touch the river from the area just above Horseshoe Lake north to the hot springs near Childs. A few roads lead to the western bank, but they are generally for four-wheel-drive vehicles.

Lake Pleasant

Lake Pleasant's 3500 surface acres make it the largest close-by lake to the Greater Phoenix area. It is not surrounded by high mountains like those that shelter the other lakes, so the prevailing southwest wind provides perfect sailing breezes. The blue bosom of Pleasant is dotted with sails on winter and spring weekends.

Named for Carl Pleasant, the engineer who designed the dam, the lake contains largemouth bass, white bass, channel catfish, crappie, and the always present sunfish and carp. The bass, largemouth and white, are most actively pursued. The usual spring-summer-fall pattern takes precedence for the largemouths.

The Agua Fria River is the main stream that feeds the lake, but there are a number of drainages. These include Cole's, Castle Creek, and Humbug, plus three or four others that also contribute water during runoff periods. The presence of occasional water in these drainages means inundated trees and bushes sometimes provide perfect places for young fish to hide. Add shallow bays for spawning, and you have a very productive piece of water.

White bass are school fish. They spawn in late winter to early spring, and the March-to-May period finds them active and vulnerable. Threadfin shad are the main forage fish in the lake, and when a school of shad is herded to the top and savaged by a school of white bass it is an awesome sight. The water boils as the tiny shad try to flee, only to be chopped to bits by the maurauding whites. Any lure thrown into the melee means an instant strike. If you're in the right place at the right time and one of these "boils" erupts within casting distance, you are an instant white-bass expert.

Pleasant is about twenty-five miles northwest of Phoenix off State Route 74. Elevation is 1500 feet, so temperatures equal those of Phoenix. The Maricopa County Parks Department is the landlord for the facilities. There is an entrance fee that allows the use of three paved launch/park areas, picnic areas (camping is available at an extra fee) and access to the marina, which offers most services.

Lower Lake Pleasant is now closed, as construction begins on new Waddell Dam, designed to make Pleasant the storage reservoir for CAP water from the Colorado River. The lake will be much larger, contain striped bass, and the level will fluctuate more than one hundred vertical feet yearly. It's too early to tell what effect this will have on fishing.

Hunting Central Arizona

Wildlife thrives in Arizona, despite the ever-growing population. Witness the excellent hunting available to those who live in central Arizona. The more than a million residents of this area have only a short drive to hunt deer, elk, javelina, antelope, bear, mountain lion, turkey, quail, rabbit, squirrel, dove, bandtail pigeon, and waterfowl.

One reason for this diversity: the region is a mini-map of Arizona. It includes desert, high pine country, and the rich chaparral of the transition zone. The area north and east of metropolitan Phoenix represents a wide range of habitat — and everything from kangaroo rats to the lordly elk.

There are those who chafe at Arizona's big-game hunting requirements. Prospective big-game hunters must enter a drawing and choose a particular unit, and the unit has a quota. If the computer doesn't issue out your name, you end up with a leftover permit for some less desirable area, or none at all.

But the deer-hunt units just north of Phoenix are a good illustration of why hunter distribution, which is what the permit system achieves, is necessary. Back in the early 1960s, before permits were required, more than 10,000 hunters annually chased deer in Unit 21. Both the quality of the hunt and the deer herd suffered. These days the same unit carries 1000 to 1500 permits in each of two separate seasons, and success figures pretty well parallel the statewide averages.

Small-game hunting is excellent, depending a bit on winter moisture. Long, liberal seasons mean small-game hunters can be afield every day of the year.

Deer Hunting

Major deer-hunting units include 21, 22, and 23, with smaller portions of 20B and 24A. They're close to the major population center, and when hunters go afield for quail or dove they often see deer as well. So many choose that area when it's time to apply for a deer permit. There are seldom leftover permits.

Hunts begin in late October and, in some units, may be layered. That is, an early four-day hunt will be authorized for 1000 hunters, let's say, then the unit will close for the rest of the week. A second hunt, with about the same number of permits, will then open for a ten-day period. This method means fewer hunters in the field at one time and a better quality outdoor experience.

Both **mule deer** and **whitetail** are found here, with the smaller whitetails at higher elevations of the desert ranges or in the pine-spruce-fir habitat in the northern parts of Units 22 and 23. There is a late hunt, usually held in December, for whitetails only in these units.

Deer numbers have been generally up in these units, reflecting several years of good moisture and good food supplies. It's not difficult early or late in the day to see deer on a drive down any back country road in these areas.

Elk Hunting

There are limited elk hunts in the fall in Units 22 and 23. These areas, below the Mogollon Rim, are on the edge of good elk habitat, but there are resident herds and a few dozen animals are taken each year. Concentrations of elk are directly at the base of the Rim, down toward Young, and over near the Fort Apache Indian Reservation.

Antelope Hunting

Unit 21 is the only piece of antelope country in this region. Most of these fleet animals are in the upper half of the unit, from Dugas north toward the Verde River. About twenty-five permits are issued annually, and ten times that many hunters apply. Antelope are open country animals, relying on speed and keen eyesight for protection, so finding them is not a problem. As is usual during antelope hunts, success figures are high: something on the order of two out of three.

Turkey Hunting

There are two turkey hunts in this region, one in the fall and one in the spring. Units 22 and 23 hold the turkey populations. Unit 22's birds are just below the Rim, and those in 23 are sprinkled throughout the high country from the Rim to the Sierra Ancha.

The fall hunt is unrestricted. You can buy a turkey tag and hunt anywhere. Hunter numbers in these areas don't approach those in the better units atop the Rim, but both 22 and 23 are popular turkey areas. Fall hunters generally bag turkeys born earlier in the year, so success depends on what kind of turkey crop has been raised.

Turkeys have a strong flock instinct. If you can find a bunch that has been spooked and scattered, it's relatively easy, with an artificial call, to lure one up close. Still, they are wary birds, and success figures are low. Only one in nine or ten hunters will score.

The spring hunt, which coincides with the nesting period, requires a permit and is for gobblers only. About 200 to 400 permits have been issued for Units 22 and 23 in recent years. Success figures pretty well parallel those of the fall hunt. Hunters may stalk gobblers after hearing them call, but the favorite method is using an artificial call to challenge the gobbler, thus enticing him within range. This probably represents the most difficult hunt, outside of going for lion or bear.

Bear Hunting

A few bears are taken annually from Unit 21, generally in the northern part, above the Verde River breaks. Unit 22 is better bear country. The Mazatzal Wilderness Area along the Verde holds good numbers of bears but is rough, thickly grown, and tough to hunt. No motorized vehicles are

Hunting

allowed, so it's walk or ride a horse. There are bears just under the Rim and down into the chaparral country as far south as Sunflower. In fact, when the prickly-pear fruit is ripe, usually in September, the bears will come to the high desert to gorge on this rich diet.

Unit 23 is one of the better bear areas in the state. Nearly the entire unit, except the desert country just north of Roosevelt Lake, is bear habitat. The bruins like the rough, brushy country found here. It offers a wide variety of food, plenty of cover, varied terrain, and almost no people. September and October are favorite hunting months. Patient work with binoculars will find bear; so will the use of a predator call. Packs of hounds also are useful.

Lion Hunting

Because of the great abundance of misinformation circulated about the mountain lion, also known as cougar or puma, many non-hunters (and a good many hunters too) believe this animal is in danger of disappearing. On the contrary, records show that in Arizona, at least, there are about as many lions now as there were twenty or thirty years ago, in excess of 1500. About two hundred are taken each year by hunters but they inhabit the thickest, wildest, most rugged areas of the state and they have successfully resisted several efforts, mounted earlier in the century, to reduce their numbers drastically because of depradations on game and cattle. They do, indeed, kill and eat deer and elk but studies show that food supplies and habitat, rather than lion predation, are normally the controlling factors in deer and elk populations. Mountain lions are solitary, territorial animals, usually spending the majority of their time in the thickest, roughest, least populated portions of their range. Sighting a lion in the wild is a rare and thrilling experience.

All five units represented in this region contain good numbers of lions, although "good" is a relative term when it comes to these secretive animals. The total number of lions taken during a recent year — counting all five units — was less than two dozen.

The rough chaparral country is prime lion habitat and this region has that kind of cover in abundance. Units 22 and 23 are the top areas. Most of the lions are taken by professional hunters with dogs.

Javelina Hunting

Hunting for this desert-dwelling peccary is by permit only, and all five units represented have javelina populations. Hunts are held in early March, when desert temperatures are pleasant. In recent years, Units 20B and 23 have been restricted to handguns and muzzleloaders with 21 and 22 open to regular firearms. All units in this region are open for archery hunting in January with no special permit needed. Success figures are generally in the twenty to twenty-five

percent category for firearms and slightly less for archers.

Javelina are occasionally found at surprisingly high elevations, but the bulk of the population is confined to desert and chaparral areas, the lower part of Units 21, 22, and 23 and all of 20B and 24B.

Small-Game Hunting

Gambel's quail attract more hunters than any other single species of game. They are most prevalent in low country but may occur anywhere from the desert on up into chaparral and juniper. Populations depend on nesting success, which in turn depends on winter and early spring rains. Hunting has little effect on overall bird numbers, so the season runs from early October to mid-February and the bag limits are liberal.

Desert areas with thick cover, adjacent to cultivated fields, are always a good bet, as are areas around desert water holes, along washes, and in the vicinity of the Salt and Verde River reservoirs and Lake Pleasant. The Tonto Basin, north of Roosevelt Lake, is always a hot spot.

Both **mourning dove** and **whitewing dove** are important game birds in this region, and two hunts are held each year. Both birds are legal game during the September season. The whitewings migrate to Mexico in late August-early September, so the late hunt in December-January is for mourning doves only. Some desert areas hold decent numbers of birds, especially around water holes. But the bulk of the good shooting is near agricultural areas, particularly in the Chandler-Queen Creek district.

Crop changes and the loss of habitat along the river courses have affected the dove supply, so it really isn't as good as it was "in the good old days." But we still have wing shooting here that is the envy of shotgun hunters in other states. There's no doubt the dove hunts will continue to be among the most popular outdoor events of the year.

Bandtail pigeons inhabit the upper reaches of Units 20B, 21, 22, and 23, from areas just below the Rim south to oak-juniper habitat. These birds migrate, too, and in some years most of the bandtails disappear by the October opening. Acorns are a major food item, so check oak thickets, especially those near water holes or lakes where the pigeons like to cluster in the tops of dead trees. Bandtails are tough, fast-flying targets. Collecting a limit is a real and heady challenge.

The **Abert squirrel** is found in the upper reaches of Units 22 and 23, in open, park-like areas of ponderosa pine. Aberts are most active on calm, sunny days. You'll see them on the ground as often as in the pines, although they head for the tallest, thickest part of the tree when alarmed. The October-November season often is a period of crisp, clear days in Arizona's high country.

Waterfowl hunting in this region can be good for those

who are willing to do some traveling, some walking, and don't mind days when no shots are fired at all. Major lakes in the area hold **ducks** and **geese.** Roosevelt Lake has a refuge on the Tonto arm and several thousand Canada geese winter there, often flying out to feed early and late in the day. Both Tonto Creek and the Salt River above the lake hold ducks and (sometimes) geese. The Bartlett-Horseshoe area also has some resident geese and ducks during winter months, and the Agua Fria, above Lake Pleasant, always holds ducks, with an occasional small flock of geese.

Stock watering ponds in desert areas may have ducks or geese for a few days, when migrating flocks drop in to rest or feed, and "jump shooting" is a popular way to prospect for waterfowl. By sneaking up to the edge of the water holes, you can get shots as the ducks jump into the air.

The Verde River is a good duck and goose location, but accessible areas are hunted hard all the way from Bartlett upstream to Camp Verde. Hunters who walk up or down-stream from access points may get good shooting, mostly of the "jump" variety.

Hunting in this low country tends to be best late in the season as northern birds head south to escape storms and winter freeze-ups of lakes and ponds. It really gets into gear in December and improves weekly until the end of the season in January.

Cottontail rabbits are abundant in desert regions, especially in the thick cover adjacent to irrigated farmlands and around desert water holes. There's no closed season, and daily limits are liberal. Combining ready availability and good-on-the-table qualities, rabbits are among the most popular game animals in the state.

Mourning doves

The San Carlos Reservation

It's big and lonesome. Nearly two million acres of the San Carlos Indian Reservation stretch from Mount Turnbull on the south, across the Gila River, and up the gently sloping grassland to the Natanes Plateau. Then there is a wide swath of oak-juniper-pine forest, a swoop into the canyon that holds the Black River, and, after its meeting with the White, the even deeper gorge of the Salt River.

Nearly all the Apache of the San Carlos tribe live in the town of San Carlos or in one of the small communities along U. S. Route 70 which runs through the southern part of the reservation. A few cowboys live on scattered ranches, and during summer months a forest fire crew and a game warden live at Point of Pines. The rest of the huge reservation is occupied only by wildlife, cattle, and memories.

If you take Apache Route 10 east from the smooth pavement of U. S. Route 60 north of Globe, you can drive for 150 miles across the reservation, past Point of Pines and south on Apache Route 15 to Clifton and Morenci without seeing a gas station, a telephone, or maybe even another vehicle. The main route to Point of Pines is suitable for any sort of vehicle in dry weather, but most unpaved roads on

the reservation are best tackled with a high-clearance vehicle. A majority of the smaller side roads require four-wheel-drive capability in any sort of weather.

So it takes a spirit of adventure to leave the familiar trappings of civilization and plunge off into the wild country of the San Carlos Apache. The land itself is neutral, neither threatening nor friendly. It reflects your attitude.

If you enter the San Carlos well-supplied and self-contained, perhaps traveling with a companion vehicle as an extra margin of safety, you'll enjoy the solitude, the excellent fishing, the good hunting, and the chance to camp in uncrowded surroundings. Your San Carlos experience will be one to remember.

But if you take off into the interior of the reservation with no map, no plan, and no knowledge of the possible difficulties, that experience could be unforgettable in a very different way.

The lure of the San Carlos preserve is irresistible. Tell an angler that nearly 200 small ponds on the huge reservation hold trout or catfish, that the hatchery truck driver sprinkles rainbows here and there—and no one knows for sure, from year to year, which ponds are best—then try to stop him from trying his luck.

Javelina hunters on the San Carlos reservation average three times the success figure in the rest of the state. And bear hunters who walk along the Black River for a mile are sure to see a fresh track.

Because recreation is an economic resource, the San Carlos Apache charge fees for fishing, hunting, and camping. The fees are not high—about the price of a movie ticket for a day of fishing, for example—but this does tend to keep visitor numbers down, especially when combined with the lack of development in much of the Apache's territory. Generally, the fees represent an excellent value in view of the potential returns.

Huge San Carlos Lake is one of the top largemouth bass waters in the West, catfishing is excellent and crappies sometimes top the four pound mark. If you can't catch fish here—you can't catch fish!

San Carlos recreation is now under the jurisdiction of a professional wildlife biologist and a five-man commission of young, aggressive Apaches who set policy, so look for continued development of the tribe's outdoor resources and a slow, steady improvement in facilities and services.

Those who take the time to get acquainted with the San Carlos Apache find them cordial and intelligent, with a fine sense of humor. They are proud of their beautiful homeland and anxious to share its beauty with visitors.

The rugged back country of the San Carlos reservation is not for everyone. But for the breed that aches to see where the dim road leads, that is more interested in the pursuit than the catch, and whose imagination takes flight with the appearance of the evening star, this is the place.

(Above left) Nantack Ridge in the Natanes Mountains, west of Point of Pines. Jerry Jacka

(Right) Every muscle taut, a mountain lion silently stalks its prey. Lions traverse remote reaches of the San Carlos reservation, but few are taken in any year. Bill McRae

(Above) Trout from one of the tiny ponds in the northern part of the San Carlos Indian Reservation. Bob Hirsch

(Left) San Carlos Lake, sometimes called Coolidge Reservoir by old-timers, is one of the best largemouth bass producers in the state. Jerry Jacka

(Below) The lake is famous for crappies, too, and there's a lot of excitement every spring when the great speckled beauties come up into the shallows. Bob Hirsch

145

(Left) Turkeys are found primarily in the high country in the northeastern portion of the reservation. Judd Cooney

(Below left) The collared peccary, better known as javelina or just wild pig. The San Carlos hunt is one of the best in Arizona. Norm Smith

(Below) Among the prickly pear and desert shrubs you might scare up a covey of Gambel's quail. Paul Berquist

(Bottom) Both the lake and some of the small ponds on the reservation are good spots for Canada geese. James Tallon

(Following panel, pages 148-149) The vast Sonoran Desert rings with the plaintive morning call of Gambel's quail. Larry Toschik

Region 8

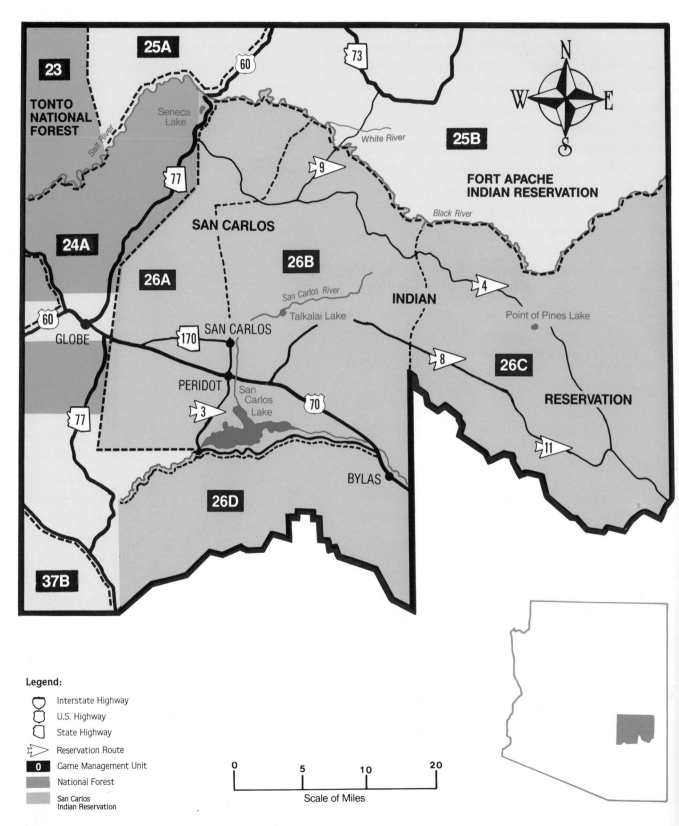

Legend:

- Interstate Highway
- U.S. Highway
- State Highway
- Reservation Route
- **0** Game Management Unit
- National Forest
- San Carlos Indian Reservation

Scale of Miles

0   5   10   20

Fishing the San Carlos Reservation

Anglers on the huge San Carlos Indian Reservation have two choices—big water or little water—and each offers a distinctive adventure.

The big water is San Carlos Lake. The old-timers call it Coolidge Reservoir, from the name of the dam on the Gila River that impounds the sprawling, 18,000-acre body of water. The dam was built in the late 1920s as storage for irrigation water for farmers in the Florence area. The construction was a major event, and the odd design (the dam looks a little like a series of eggs standing on end, side by side) caused a good deal of comment.

President Calvin Coolidge came for the formal dedication, but although the dam was finished, no water had backed up behind it. The Gila had shrunk to a tiny trickle, and the bottom of the lake was full of grazing cattle. Will Rogers accompanied the President and when it was his time to speak, he told the crowd: "If this was my lake, I'd mow it!"

The lake eventually did catch water and provide irrigation. But it was fifty years before the lake finally filled, and in that half-century, the water level varied from high to empty. The fish population was repeatedly wiped out and restocked, and with each restocking, the population boomed. There would be a few years of extraordinary fishing, and then the inevitable draw-down would occur. The fish would die, fisheries biologists would wait for a new water supply, and the cycle would begin again.

In great contrast to the big reservoir is the other half of the San Carlos fishing facilities—ponds and lakes.

Sprinkled across the reservation's nearly two million acres are dozens of small ponds, built as cattle-watering places. A bulldozer pushes an earthen dam across a small wash or drainage to catch rain or, in the higher parts of the reservation, snowmelt.

These tiny impoundments are called tanks in the West, and they vary from less than one-fourth acre in size to as large as fifty acres or so, although the average is more like one or two surface acres. Tanks in the higher parts of the reservation are stocked with rainbow trout, with channel catfish sometimes added, and an occasional brown trout. The lower ponds, too warm for trout, are typically stocked with catfish.

The Apache have built three lakes solely for recreation in the past few years. They are Talkalai, Point of Pines, and Seneca lakes. The Black River, with its wilderness fishing for smallmouth bass, trout, and catfish, forms the northern boundary of the reservation, and the San Carlos Apache share its bounty with the White Mountain Apache Tribe. There are a number of popular access points from the San Carlos side of the river.

To fish the San Carlos, you'll pay a fee, a small daily charge or a yearly permit. You also need a permit daily or yearly to put your boat on any of the reservation waters. In both cases, the charges are low enough so the money spent represents one of the best outdoor bargains ever, your passport to a huge land of fishing opportunity.

San Carlos Lake

San Carlos Lake still operates under the boom-and-bust philosophy: The lake's water supply and the quality of the fishing depend on the downstream irrigators. The lake is wide and shallow, with dozens of coves of flooded brush. A regular load of nutrients from the Gila River, perfect spawning conditions, and the ample cover guarantee that a higher-than-normal percentage of the young fish will survive. Add a year-long growing season, and the result is explosive growth that can literally pave the lake with bass, crappie, catfish, and bluegills.

Yes, there are days when the fish refuse to cooperate, just as there are on any piece of water anywhere. But generally, San Carlos ranks near the top of Arizona lakes as a consistent producer of fish—lots of fish, and big fish as well. Two long-standing records attest to the big-fish claim. In 1951 a 65-pound flathead catfish was taken here, and it has held the record ever since. A crappie taken in 1959 is also an unbeaten champ: it weighed four pounds, ten ounces. But even that record could fall from this super-producer.

You can catch fish on San Carlos any day of the year, but the best action for bass begins about March and continues through April, May, and June. Bass fishing stays good to excellent right through the summer, although the 2500-foot elevation means daytime temperatures over 100 degrees, and that discourages some anglers. The fall months remain good, with some outstanding top water action. The bass tend to retreat to deeper water during the December-March period, but skillful, patient fishermen catch the largest fish of the year at this time.

Crappie move into the shallows to begin their spawning activity in March, and big strings of the great speckled beauties are taken from then until mid-May, with occasional good catches again in the fall.

Both flathead and channel catfish provide good sport and good eating for San Carlos anglers. Warmer water triggers hotter fishing, and nights are generally better than days. San Carlos is almost always murky—sometimes downright muddy—and under that condition, the whiskered clan feeds 24 hours per day. Best bets are May through September, and the lake contains some real tackle smashers.

Access to the lake is via U.S. Route 70, about twenty miles east of Globe. Good, graded roads lead to a number of camp/launch sites at various places around the lake. Soda Canyon, Mohave Point, County Line, and Blue Cove are some of the most popular. There is a store with picnic supplies, tackle and bait at Soda Canyon, near the dam. Campers need to be self-contained, though most areas have ramadas, pit toilets and garbage cans.

Fishing

Talkalai Lake

Talkalai Lake is the newest Apache impoundment. It's on the San Carlos River, just a few miles northeast of the community of San Carlos, which is tribal headquarters. With 200 surface acres, Talkalai is not a big lake, but already there are legends circulating about the awesome power of its catfish — probably huge flatheads. Anglers are hooking some kind of big fish, but the battles are short; the fish simply take off and are unstoppable. Add largemouth bass, crappie, and bluegill and you have super fishing possibilities.

The special bass limit here is five fish per day, rather than the ten allowed elsewhere on the reservation. Outboard motors to eight horsepower are allowed. There are a number of places to launch small boats; a surfaced ramp is on the south shore, uplake from the dam. A number of ramadas are sprinkled around the lake — no other facilities.

Point of Pines Lake

Point of Pines Lake is another fairly recent addition. It's in the pines about three miles west of Point of Pines, a small collection of cabins that serves as a base for forest fire crews during the summer months. The lake is about twenty-seven surface acres and contains rainbow trout. There's a small campground here, but no other facilities. Access roads are unpaved but generally suitable for all types of vehicles. Like most Arizona trout waters, Point of Pines is best early and late in the year. It is stocked regularly, and catching some pan-size rainbows usually is fairly easy.

Seneca Lake

Seneca Lake is just off U. S. Route 60, about thirty miles northeast of Globe. The twenty-five-acre lake is nearly surrounded by cattails, so a boat is a big help. Seneca contains trout, largemouth bass, and catfish, plus a population of bluegills. The trout are stocked and bite best from November to March, with some nice carryover fish the rest of the year. The bass and catfish are most often caught in spring, summer, and fall. There are camping and picnic areas around the lake and a small store that sells permits.

Stock Tanks

The small stock tanks, which are sprinkled throughout the reservation and may number 150 to 200, generally hold channel catfish if in the lower elevations, and rainbow trout if in the northern, juniper-pine areas.

Which trout tanks are stocked and when depends on the supply of both money and water. Fish for the San Carlos reservation come from the federal hatchery at Williams Creek on the Fort Apache reservation, and supplies fluctuate with budgets. Some tanks have water every year, some only when rain and snowmelt are heavy.

Apache Routes 10, 9, and 4 traverse the northern part of the San Carlos from U. S. Route 60 on the west to Point of Pines on the east, and pretty well split the trout area. Tanks north and south of the road within a five- to ten-mile swath are generally stocked with trout, and occasionally the same tanks also contain catfish. But not all the tanks have trout, and even impoundments that hold trout one year may not have them the next.

An angler tries his luck on San Carlos Lake as the sun announces a new day. Bob Hirsch

Add generally poor roads that demand at least a pickup-type vehicle and often are for four-wheel-drive only, and you get the idea that fishing on the San Carlos reservation, away from the lakes specifically designed for recreation, is very "iffy." *If* the roads are suitable, *if* trout have been stocked, *if* you can find the individual tank you're searching for, and *if* the fish decide to bite, you might come home with some trout. The catfish picture is a bit more reliable.

Still, rumors circulate about some angler's finding a tiny tank that was stocked three years before and has never been fished since.

Warning: The back country of the San Carlos has no phones, no gas, no drinking water, and no towns. Once you leave the pavement, you're on your own. If your vehicle breaks down, it could be weeks before someone comes along. The best bet is to travel in pairs and let someone know where you're going and when you plan to return.

Black River

Black River winds its crooked way along the northern boundary of the San Carlos reservation. From where it meets the Apache Sitgreaves National Forest, in the country near Malay Gap, downstream to the pump station north of Point of Pines, the Black River is a trout stream. Some smallmouth bass are found in the lower reaches of this stretch, but rainbows are the main objective. A few browns

are sprinkled among the rapids and the long, deep pools.

From the pump station to Black River Crossing, where Apache Route 9 crosses the river on a bridge, the smallmouth bass reigns. There are some good channel cats in the big pools, and the farther downstream, the better the chances of catching them.

The bridged crossing just mentioned is the only one on the Black River from Wildcat, just south of Big Lake, to the bridge on U. S. Route 60 at the bottom of Salt River Canyon. So for more than one hundred miles, the Black winds through some of the wildest, most remote, most inaccessible country in the state. A few roads, four-wheel-drive only, touch the river from the San Carlos side. A few more run out to the edge of the canyon that holds the river, and anglers can hike down to the water. There are a few spots where you can begin at one road, backpack down the river, and arrange to be picked up at another spot.

Smallmouth fishing is best in May and June, before summer rains can turn the clear water into a good imitation of chocolate milk. There's another good period in October, before the winter snows arrive. Because access is so limited, the Black is lightly fished, and the smallmouths are unsophisticated in the remote sections. Almost any lure will bring a strike. But it's impossible to overstate the ruggedness of the area. The Black River is no place for the timid or unprepared.

Crappie

Hunting the San Carlos Reservation

The San Carlos Indian Reservation is very large and mostly undeveloped—just the sort of situation that appeals to hunters. The big-game list includes deer, elk, bear, javelina, lion, and predators, but permit numbers are limited. Special fees discourage many hunters, so competition is generally light. Small game include quail, squirrel, and waterfowl; the fee for a yearly license is an excellent value.

With few exceptions, reservation roads are suitable only for high-clearance vehicles, and most of the back-country roads are four-wheel-drive only. U. S. Route 70 extends through the reservation, and the road to the Point of Pines area (Apache Route 8) is suitable for any sort of vehicle, but on most other roads, the hunter needs to be self-sufficient and well equipped.

If you are ready to tackle some wild country and put forth some extra effort, hunting opportunities are excellent.

Deer Hunting

The reservation has some mule deer, mostly in the low country, but hunts are a sometimes thing, authorized only occasionally. There are more whitetails, the Coues species, including some record-book heads. A tightly controlled trophy-type hunt for these deer may be authorized from time to time.

Decisions on whether to authorize deer permits, and if so, how many and for what portions of the reservation, are made early in the year. When available, permits are issued on a first-come basis.

Elk Hunting

There's a resident herd of elk in the high country of the northern part of the reservation and winter storms can also trigger a migration of elk across the Black River from the White Mountain Apache reservation. Some very large elk are taken here and a limited permit trophy hunt is held each winter. There are huge elk in a number of places in Arizona—the San Carlos reservation contributes its share. The trophy hunt is not inexpensive but considering the possible rewards, it's still a bargain.

Turkey Hunting

The Apache have good numbers of turkey on the high, pine-covered plateau that parallels the Black River in the northern half of the reservation. Dozens of the stock tanks sprinkled here and there in the pines seem to have a resident flock and summer camper/fishermen are often awakened by the natural alarm clock of a flock of the big birds coming to water at dawn. There is usually a limited permit hunt in the fall and again in the spring and both offer a chance to hunt undisturbed turkeys, birds that have not been spooked by some other hunter.

Bear Hunting

The tribe authorizes a bear hunt in the spring and another in the fall, both are very popular with Arizona bear hunters. The rugged country along the Black River is prime bear habitat. Some hunters simply use binoculars to check out the canyonsides on drainages along the Black. Others lure the bear within range by using a predator call that imitates the distress cry of a terrified rabbit. Originally designed to attract coyotes, bobcats, and other predators, the squalling sound also works with bears and is widely used in the thick, up-and-down canyon country along the river. Apache wardens estimate fifty to sixty bears are taken annually on the reservation.

Javelina Hunting

An unlimited number of permits is made available for the archery javelina season, usually held the first two weeks of January. The rolling grassland in the southern half of the reservation is excellent javelina habitat, and success is always high. The reservation is divided into four hunt sites, and javelina hunting is sometimes allowed in all four, sometimes in three, with one of the units closed for a year or two.

The firearms javelina hunt is held in March, and it has a limited number of permits. Sixty to seventy percent success is common, and one year, in the unit south of San Carlos Lake, every hunter took a javelina.

Small-Game Hunting

The San Carlos has populations of three kinds of Arizona **quail**—the Gambel's, scaled, and Mearns'—but the jaunty, top-knotted Gambel's predominates. The Apache lay on a yearly fee for small-game hunting and that discourages enough hunters that you seldom have much competition. There are occasional coveys of Gambel's in the oak-pine cover atop the Natanes Plateau, but the majority of the birds are found in the rolling grassland and broken canyon country on the southern two-thirds of the huge reservation. The shoreline areas of San Carlos Lake always hold birds and if you happen to have both fishing and hunting permits, it's sometimes tough to decide which to do. If you're sitting in a boat fishing for bass and two dozen quail stream noisily down a slope to the water's edge, it's tempting to swap the rod for a shotgun. Or you may be busting brush on a ridge overlooking the lake, trying to find a batch of birds, when a sudden explosion of surface activity in a nearby cove on the lake means the bass are chasing shad and you should be there, right then. Most areas are suitable for pointing dogs, too, and they add greatly to the hunt—both for the enjoyment of watching them run and for ensuring that no birds are lost.

Hunting

One of the best things about quail hunting is the knowledge that hunting has no significant effect on bird numbers. The quail population waxes and wanes in concert with winter and spring rains. If they occur in the proper amounts at the proper time, there will be lots of quail in the fall. If two or three of these "good" years occur in a row, Gambel's quail hunting will be spectacular, especially in a lightly hunted area like the San Carlos. Even if the birds are unhunted, only a certain percentage will survive to the following spring.

Waterfowl hunting is best late in the season, from about mid-December to the end of the hunt. There are **ducks** and **geese** on San Carlos Lake, and there's especially good hunting for the geese when they fly out to feed early and late in the day. "Jump shooting" the stock tanks is a good way to find both ducks and geese, but it's a long way between these small pieces of water. Some of the tanks will

be "empty," not holding birds right then, and occasionally you can spend an entire day without being in the right place at the right time. The tanks in the southern half of the reservation are the best bet; those higher up will have ice or be inaccessible because of snow.

The Apache sell both a daily and yearly small-game permit that covers quail, waterfowl, and **squirrels.** The seasons are the same as those established by the Arizona Game and Fish Department. The tassel-eared Abert squirrels are found in the high ponderosa pine country, generally on both sides of Apache Routes 10 and 9 off U. S. Route 60 in the northwestern part of the San Carlos, and in the BS Gap and Malay Gap areas northeast of Point of Pines. Hunting pressure is light, and collecting enough squirrels for a big pot of stew usually is no problem.

Many hunters consider the Canada goose the ultimate waterfowl trophy. James Tallon

Southwestern Arizona

This is the dry land, the land of creosote flats between steep-sided mountain ranges, as close to the popular notion of desert as Arizona ever gets. Water is precious here, and life revolves around the wells and water holes—what the Spanish called *tinajas*. They sustain the area's wildlife and over the centuries have made the difference between life and death for ancient Indians, early day pioneers, and even those who choose to spend some time in the remote corners of this region today.

It is a land of distances. When you drive west on Interstate Route 8 from Gila Bend, the mountain ranges on the western horizon never seem to get closer; what seems thirty miles away may be five times that far.

On this somber-hued landscape, nature put two brilliant slashes of color: the blue and green courses of the Gila and

Colorado rivers. The Gila's broad floodplain is mostly farmland now. The huge forests of mesquite are gone, and the river itself is barely damp except during periods of high runoff. Man's hand has changed the Colorado, too. It is more canal than broad, rushing river; its power is tamed and contained, its water used and used and used again.

At first glance, this does not seem a place where wildlife would thrive. But God's creatures are adaptable, and this southwestern quadrant of the state offers an amazing variety. The rugged ranges look like bighorn sheep country and the creatures of the crags are here, using the sparse vegetation not only to survive but to flourish. There are deer, too, including some giant-antlered desert muleys. And along the water courses and the edges of the cropland is some of the best dove shooting in the state. The same well-watered

areas are home to Gambel's quail, the familiar top-knotted bird that is the jaunty symbol of the desert. And for those who know where and when, this may be the best place in the state to collect a limit of geese!

Except for some isolated pockets here and there, game—big and small—is not easy to find in this immense landscape. But hunting in the scattered ranges and on the paloverde flats has a special flavor, and those who taste it always return. There is a wild beauty here that is revealed to those who climb the jagged ridges, who use binoculars and spotting scopes to probe the light and shadow of a hidden basin, who believe the desert sun burns away all things non-essential.

The region offers anglers a different world, too. The Colorado nears its meeting with the Sea of Cortez here, its last two hundred miles as exciting as the first, high in the mountains of Wyoming and Colorado. There are no soaring cliffs to contain the flow. Instead, the river alternately races between levees and riprap, then meanders to create intriguing backwaters screened from view behind willows and cattails, looping oxbows that water the thirsty sand.

These areas where the river runs free are constantly changing, as when a sandbar builds at the entrance to a hidden channel, then shifts again when the flow increases. More water means new channels and new places for largemouth bass, catfish, crappies, and bluegills to hide. It's easy to get lost in the maze of twisting channels and backwaters, and in some areas every trip is a new challenge.

The lower Colorado is also the home of one of Arizona's largest species of fish—the flathead catfish. These giants of the catfish clan can reach weights of one hundred pounds. The river record keeps going up and has passed the mid-fifties. Talk to any serious angler in the area and you'll hear tales of huge fish inhaling the bait and moving away, unstoppable.

The slightly saline quality of the river's water also appeals to the tilapia, a panfish from Africa that has found a home in the river and the surrounding canals. The bluegill-shaped fish grow to five pounds or so, although the average catch is more like hand-size. They lend an additional intriguing quality to a stretch of river that is already unique.

This vast and unpeopled region is not for everyone. It is too harsh and rugged and dry, too demanding of its users, too unforgiving to the uncommitted. But for those who choose to learn its ways, it is the ultimate outdoor adventure, a return to the basic values, a land as warm as the sun that nourishes it.

(Above left) A dove hunter and her Brittany spaniel work their way across a field near Gila Bend. James Tallon

(Right) A section of the Colorado River near Parker, still a magnet to both wildlife and human populations. Jack Dykinga

(Above) A fisherman in his office, hard at work.
J. Peter Mortimer

(Right) Taylor Lake is typical of the winding backwaters along the Colorado from Parker Dam to Yuma.
Farboia-Archives

(Below) A happy fisherman with one of the big stripers that are now appearing in this section of the river.
J. Peter Mortimer

(Right) Rugged desert mountain ranges punctuate this corner of the state. Surprisingly, they support a remarkable variety of wildlife, including bighorn sheep and mule deer. Tony Mandile

(Far right) Pursuit of the agile cottontail provides countless hours afield for Arizona hunters. Judd Cooney

(Below) This is the realm of the desert bighorn, one of the rarest sheep in the world, found only in the southwestern United States and Mexico. Ernie Weegen

(Bottom right) Hunter and his dog at daybreak. The valley of the Gila River from Yuma to Gila Bend is one of the premier dove hunting areas in the nation. James Tallon

(Following panel, pages 162-163) Winter is heralded by the arrival of Canada geese from the north. Sometimes they spend the entire winter at the major waterways of the state. Larry Toschik

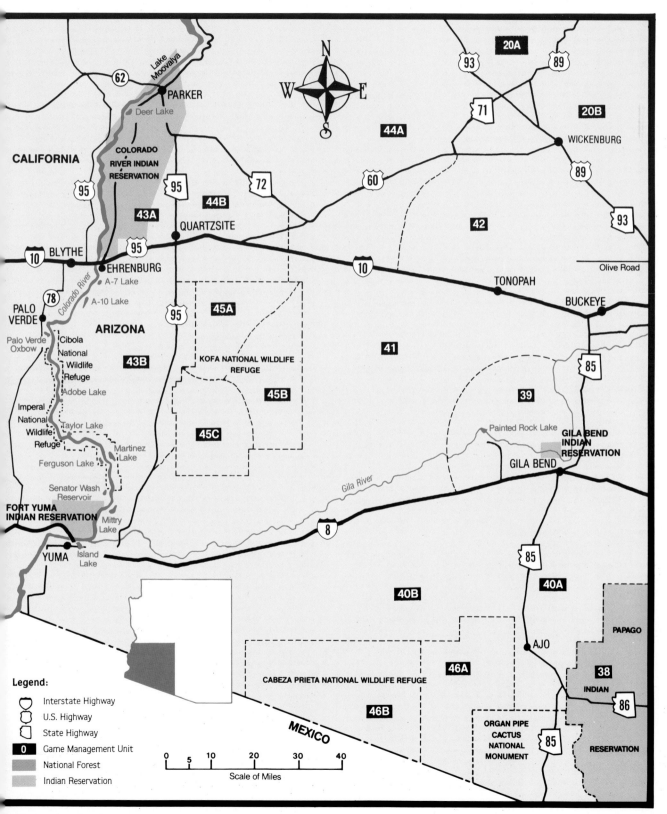

Legend:
- Interstate Highway
- U.S. Highway
- State Highway
- 0 Game Management Unit
- National Forest
- Indian Reservation

0 5 10 20 30 40
Scale of Miles

*eft) Hummingbird bush in spring bloom. Tinajas Altos
ountains form the background.* Peter Kresan

Fishing Southwestern Arizona

Challenge the average person to describe the southwestern corner of Arizona in one word and you'll get answers like "dry," "rugged," "empty," or "lonesome." If that person were a fisherman, the word likely would be "Colorado," for the Colorado River. Except for some minor fishing in canals in the Buckeye and Gila Bend areas, and occasionally in the Gila River, fishing in this portion of Arizona is all in the Colorado River or its backwaters.

For many miles, the Colorado between Parker and the Mexican border is nothing more than a broad canal lined with riprap, existing solely to transport water in the most efficient way possible. Other sections are more like the wild river the Colorado used to be. There is a main channel, to be sure, but its thickly grown banks of shrub and cattail conceal backwaters: loops and twists, small pools, and mini-lakes. They are lined by brush and reeds and are invisible until you break through the last screen of stalks and emerge into some quiet hideaway.

It's easy to get lost in the maze of mostly unmarked channels, and only long years of experience enable anglers to spot the tiny opening that might lead to an out-of-sight pond full of drowned trees and hungry bass.

This is mostly bass and catfish country. Fishermen down here don't say much, but some of the biggest largemouth bass in the state, along with maybe the best average-size stringers of bass, come from the warm, salty waters of the lower Colorado. It was here that flathead catfish were stocked back in the early 1960s. Now monster cats are being taken that weigh more than fifty pounds and measure four feet in length.

There are crappie in the shallow, brushy backwaters, and they begin to bite in January, a month or more ahead of fish in the rest of the state. Striped bass have drifted downstream from the upriver reservoirs, and they occasionally provide some wild, unexpected sport.

Anglers anticipating a strike from a largemouth in the two- or three-pound range are jolted when a twenty-pound striper engulfs the lure instead. The river and the canals that empty into it are also the home of the tilapia (till *lap*'ia), an African panfish now widely distributed in this part of Arizona. They can tolerate the warmth and salt; in fact, they thrive on it. Most tilapia are pan-size at best, but they do grow to more than four pounds, and there have been reports of five-pounders.

The Colorado is the boundary between Arizona and California. You can fish from the Arizona bank with an Arizona fishing license, but if you venture out onto the river itself, you must buy a stamp from California to be legal (Californians buy an Arizona stamp, so the program is reciprocal).

Beginning at Parker Dam and continuing south to Yuma, fishing on the Colorado looks like this:

The Parker Strip

It's about 190 miles from Parker Dam to the Mexican border, and that's a lot of water. The fifteen or so miles from the dam to the town of Parker are called the **"Parker strip"** or **Lake Moovalya.** The banks are so crowded with resorts and commercial establishments that fishing is not popular with the general public. But the locals know this stretch contains largemouth bass, bluegills, and channel catfish.

You can fish from shore or a boat. Try summer nights for catfish here. The busy boat traffic is gone, and night-crawlers, waterdogs, or anchovies will catch an occasional bass as well. The last three miles of this stretch are on the Colorado River Indian Reservation, and you'll need a tribal permit to fish.

It's about forty miles by river from **Parker to the Palo Verde diversion dam,** and the river here flows through the Colorado River Indian Reservation. In fact, the reservation continues for about ten miles below the Palo Verde dam to a point three miles above Ehrenberg. The river in this section contains largemouth bass, channel catfish, bluegills, and occasional striped bass.

There are also smallmouth bass, and the **Deer Lake area** a few miles south of Parker is one of the better smallmouth spots. The area just below the Palo Verde dam is a good smallmouth area, too, and flathead catfish begin to show from here south to Yuma.

Colorado River water is used a good many times between the mountains of Wyoming and Colorado and the Gulf of California—the Sea of Cortez—and much of the river channel on the Indian reservation is bordered by levees or riprap. Still, there is some decent fishing here, and the area gets comparatively little pressure.

From **Palo Verde dam downstream to Imperial National Wildlife Refuge,** the river is free-flowing, and there are countless backwaters and loops. **A-7 Lake** is a popular fishing spot just below the Interstate 10 bridge at Ehrenberg. It has boat access via a dirt launch ramp at the north end of the lake. Best fishing is in winter and spring, and the area gets very weedy in late summer. Some tilapia begin to show here and are found in the river south to Yuma. **A-10 Lake** is six river miles south of the bridge. The long, skinny backwater has no access from the river. You'll find lots of brush and reeds here.

Palo Verde Oxbow Lake

Palo Verde Oxbow Lake is about fifteen miles south of I-10 and it, too, has no river access. There is a dirt launch area. The U-shaped lake is fed by culvert and gate, and though it is on the California side of the river, the state line here follows the old course of the river. The Oxbow is still accessible to Arizona anglers with an Arizona license.

The Cibola Area

Cibola and Imperial National Wildlife Refuges are both open to fishing, and from Cibola Lake downstream, the river becomes a maze of backwaters and moving sand bars. These can be hazardous to boating at low water levels. There are largemouth bass, catfish (both channel and flathead), and occasional stripers in the main channels, but the best fishing is often the fingers, ponds, backwaters, and mini-lakes.

They can be difficult to locate if you don't know the territory, and the narrow, often hidden channels can change from year to year as sandbars appear or cane and reeds clog access. Sometimes the smaller ponds are completely land-locked, and the best way to fish them is to walk in from the main channel with a float tube.

Adobe, Taylor, and Island lakes are all good examples of the kind of backwaters to be found from the lower end of Cibola to Yuma. In addition to the more abundant fish species found in this section of the river, Taylor Lake gave up the state record smallmouth bass (Colorado River division) back in 1980. It weighed four and one-half pounds.

Martinez Lake

Martinez Lake is just downriver from the southern boundary of the Imperial refuge, and it has good access and full facilities for Arizona anglers. Martinez is a bass fisherman's dream, with vast, flooded flats filled with brush and dead trees, plus patches of reeds. At dusk and dawn, the area seems perfect for a top-water lure or a small, shallow-running plug that wiggles and wobbles past all those pieces of cover that obviously hold bass.

The California Side of the River

Ferguson Lake is on the western side of the river, and Arizona fishermen can try their luck there as long as they have the required California stamp on the back of their license. This is super catfish country, too, and both channel and flathead cats decorate stringers all year at Martinez.

Senator Wash Reservoir is a pump-storage lake on the California side of the river just above Imperial Dam. Even though it's landlocked, Arizonans may fish there with a California stamp, and the Bureau of Land Management has a good campground facility and launch ramp on the southern shore. Squaw Lake is nearby. The All-American Canal takes California water from the river at Imperial Dam; the **Gila Gravity Canal** begins here on the Arizona side and offers good fishing for channel catfish.

Mittry Lake

Mittry Lake is just below Imperial Dam, and it is another brushy, shallow backwater filled with excellent fish cover.

There's good fishing for largemouth bass here, plus flathead and channel cats, and some outstanding crappie fishing occurs during the late winter and early spring.

Laguna Dam is just below Mittry, and the river from there to Morales Dam, where Mexico takes over the water, is known as the **Yuma Division.** The biggest flathead catfish come from this stretch, and there are largemouth bass as well. During periods of high water, anglers occasionally take mullet, salt water dwellers that have ascended the Colorado from the Gulf.

Gila River

The Gila River meets the Colorado in this vicinity, and the lower seven to ten miles of the river represent the area's best bet for tilapia. Both the mouth of the Gila and the area where the All-American Canal re-enters the Colorado attract concentrations of threadfin shad and are favorite fishing spots for all the species found in the river.

Painted Rock Lake

Painted Rock Lake is a flood-control reservoir northwest of Gila Bend off Interstate Route 8. It's a "sometimes" lake that depends on upstream flooding on the Salt and Gila rivers for its water supply. There is always water in the borrow pit below the dam, which was formed when earth movers scooped soil to build the huge impoundment. But the water quality and/or amount at Painted Rock is so suspect that the area's fish population is posted as "not safe for human consumption." There are bass, crappie, and catfish, plus carp, goldfish, tilapia, and sunfish, so catching fish is not difficult; there's just nothing to do with them after they're caught. There is a state park at the lower lake, and camping is pleasant during the winter months.

A small boat can usually maneuver the hidden lakes of the lower Colorado better than larger craft. James Tallon

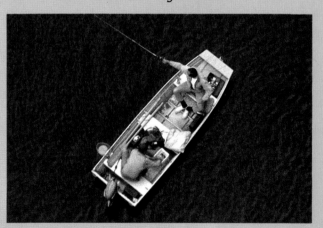

Hunting Southwestern Arizona

In the southwestern corner of Arizona, there are deer, a tiny herd of rare antelope, and small game such as waterfowl, quail, and doves. But it is the unique desert bighorn sheep that is the glamour animal of the rugged ranges.

The Gila River floodplain, which parallels Interstate 8, is developing into one long ribbon of farmland from Phoenix south and west to Yuma. But except for this man-made belt of green, the state's southwestern deserts are mostly uninhabited, studded with mountain ranges that punch up out of the flat plain like spikes on some giant war shield.

Large areas of the desert are closed to public entry because they are part of Army and Air Force proving grounds and bombing ranges. However, these areas usually are opened to sheep hunters with the proper permits and authorization.

Water is the key to survival in this arid region for both man and wildlife. This huge part of our state presents a different set of challenges to hunters, different risks, different steps to success. For most of Arizona's outdoor corps, it remains largely unknown.

Sheep Hunting

The desert bighorn sheep hunt is a good example of modern game management. Forty-four different mountain ranges in this region have sheep populations, with a total inventory of about 1800 bighorns. Only a few dozen permits are issued each year with the intent of harvesting only older, trophy rams, sheep that might be expected to be past prime breeding age and may, indeed, have only a short time to live.

Desert bighorn sheep

Two factors contribute to the success of this plan. Odds on getting drawn for a sheep permit vary from ten- or twenty-to-one to as high as 200-to-one. Thus, when a hunter spends years applying and is finally successful, he or she tends to devote a lot of time and effort to take only a large, trophy ram. The second factor parallels the first: Arizona regulations state that only one desert bighorn may be taken by a hunter. With no second chance, most hunters go into the field intending to settle for nothing but the best.

Biologists watch populations closely and issue very limited permits for specific mountain ranges. In recent years, a sportsmen's group called the Arizona Desert Bighorn Sheep Society, working with state and federal agencies, has provided labor and materials for a number of water hole projects in this region. These are designed to provide or improve desert water holes and thus open new areas for sheep habitat.

The society has also donated more than $500,000 to fund sheep transplants—a program in which bighorns are trapped and transported to mountain ranges that were once historic habitat but have not supported populations in recent times.

Some fifty bighorn permits have been issued yearly in the entire state, and about half are for this region, usually one or two to each mountain range.

Deer Hunting

In other parts of Arizona, a density of twelve deer per section of land is not unusual. In this rugged, arid region, it is six deer per section at best. Only four percent of the statewide total of deer permits are issued for this huge region. Still, about three to four percent of the harvest is accounted for from these desert ranges. And although there is more country with fewer deer, the herds contain about the same percentages of trophy bucks as deer populations elsewhere. So some big-antlered mule deer are taken each fall from ranges like the Kofas, the Harquahalas, and the Trigos.

Long-term success is at about sixteen percent, substantially less than the statewide figure of twenty to twenty-four percent. Most of the hunters who bring home venison year after year are locals who take the time to learn the country and the home range and habits of individual deer herds. There are no "hot spots"; all hunt units in this region have approximately the same hunter concentrations and general success figures.

Small-Game Hunting

There's some good to excellent waterfowl hunting along the Colorado and Gila rivers, especially when high water flows have flooded old river channels and backwaters along the Colorado, or flows in the Gila have left potholes along

that stream's course from Gila Bend to Yuma. Some parts of the Gila are surrounded by thickets of mesquite and salt cedar, so access is difficult. However, the river does hold good numbers of **ducks** and **geese,** especially late in the season. Both the Cibola and Imperial wildlife refuges harbor large flocks of geese, with as many as 20,000 Canadas at Cibola during the winter months. Having that many geese—both Canadas and snows—that close can do strange things to goose fans. One hunter studied the flights that left from the refuge each day, as the geese flew out to agricultural areas to feed. He noted one flyway was close to the top of a small mountain. Yes, he climbed the peak in the chilly hours of pre-dawn and enjoyed some top-flight pass shooting at Canada geese before the birds caught on and changed their pattern. Another hunter was also a farmer, and when one of his alfalfa fields was ready to cut he threw caution (and money!) to the winds and flooded the field instead. He lost his crop of hay but enjoyed some outstanding goose shooting.

Rabbit hunting is good along the borders of cropland where hay or grain fields abut desert cover, around desert water holes, and along washes and old canals.

Mourning dove populations are holding up well, and there is fair to good shooting for **whitewings** early in the September season, before these larger birds migrate to Mexico for the winter. The agricultural areas from Yuma to Gila Bend hold good numbers of birds. They nest and roost in the Gila River bottom and fly out to feed.

The same conditions exist on the Colorado from Yuma north to Parker, including the Colorado River Indian Reservation, where small-game hunting permits are available. Most of the shooting is done the first week in September. The remainder of the early hunt and most of the December-January season get relatively little pressure. Hunters average about four trips per year and take home five birds on each outing.

Quail hunting is for Gambel's, the familiar top-knotted species. Although numbers here seldom equal populations in the central part of the state, several consecutive years of ample rainfall can produce abundant crops of birds. Some desert foothill country has decent numbers of birds, particularly if the area is well watered, but the bulk of the hunting is along the river courses and the edges of cropland. The thickets along the Colorado and Gila rivers always have big coveys of Gambel's, but hunting is impossible; you'll hear a lot of birds fly but seldom see any targets.

Region 10

Southeastern Arizona

Here is a different Arizona. The southeastern corner of our state is a land of mountain ranges rising abruptly from rolling grassland, like tall islands in a heaving sea. Tucson crowds the south flanks of the Catalinas, the Huachuca Mountains look down on Sierra Vista and the Pinalenos on Safford, but generally these bulky ranges stand alone and uncluttered. Roads tentatively jab at their underparts and occasionally some two-track winds through the mountain over a low pass, but for the most part, paved roads and southern Arizona mountains seldom get acquainted.

This means you'll need at least a pickup and more likely a four-wheel-drive vehicle if you want to visit the roughest, wildest parts of the Galiuros, Winchesters, Santa Teresas, Dragoons, Whetstones, Chiricahuas, or any of the other mountain ranges in this region.

It is hunters who most often use the faint roads to the high basins to look for the diminutive Coues whitetail deer, perhaps to search for bear or lion, or to find a canyon that holds a herd of javelina.

In the foothills south and east of Tucson, among the tall grass and oak trees, live the Mearns' quail, birds that match the beauty of the quiet landscape. "Fool's quail," the early settlers called them, because the Mearns' choose to sit tight and be overlooked, rather than flee when danger threatens. These days, they still sit tight, so you need a good pointing dog to find them. But when they explode into flight out of their hiding places and dodge around the nearest oak, sometimes too quickly for the hunter even to raise his shotgun, nobody calls them fools.

Fishing waters in this region are few but well used. For example, some of the lakes south of Tucson, close by the

Mexican border, delight anglers in the late spring, summer, and early fall months with catches of largemouth bass, catfish, crappie, and bluegill. Then, as the waters cool, monthly stocks of pan-size rainbow trout add another species. With a little luck—an indispensible ingredient on all fishing trips—it's possible to catch fish whenever you're ready to try.

The lakes here are small but very scenic, and each has a definite personality. Peña Blanca's intriguing fifty acres wind through a narrow canyon bordered by oak-covered ridges and outcroppings of buff granite that delight the eye. Dawn lights the surrounding hills for a long time before it flows down to the lake and illuminates the whitened branches of a long-dead tree, surprised by the rising waters when the lake was built. Rucker Canyon is a clear pool reflecting the rugged peaks of the Chiricahuas, a small oval lake that, like a prom queen, enjoys its moment of glory in the spring and early summer. Then the lake's water temperature heats up and trout can no longer be stocked.

As in the state as a whole, there is great diversity in this region. You can drive from Tucson to Florence along U. S. Route 89 and see green, thickly grown desert that is home to an amazing range of flora and fauna. The latter include javelina, coyotes, foxes, rabbits, and mule deer—deer with big bodies and wide antlers, a testament to the abundant food supply.

You can take an unhurried drive from Sonoita south to Parker Canyon Lake, through the tall grass and taller oaks, and know without doubt that a Coues deer buck is resting on one of the hillsides watching you pass by.

Or you can take the Swift Trail up the long flanks of the Pinalenos while falling a little more in love with the mountain on every curve and new vista. If you're breathless when you top out and reach Riggs Flat, blame it on the 9000-foot elevation and the excitement of knowing that you'll surely catch some rainbow trout.

If this region has a best time for anglers and hunters, it is fall and winter, with their sharp, clear days and nippy nights, the kind of weather that demands you spend some time outdoors in this corner of Arizona.

(Above left) Southeastern Arizona has the finest whitetail deer hunting in the state. Some of the best areas have had success ratios of thirty to forty percent. Ron Hancock

(Right) Soaring upthrusts like the Pinaleno Mountains are forested islands in a sea of rolling grassland. Gill Kenny

(Above) An occasional largemouth bass is caught at Roper Lake State Park. Tony Mandile

(Left) Riggs Flat Lake, one of the few trout lakes in this region, is tucked away at the top of Mount Graham at an elevation of more than 8000 feet. Jerry Sieve

(Below) Relaxed fishing on Parker Canyon Lake. Pat O'Brien

(Left) Panoramic view of the Chiricahua Wilderness.
David Muench

(Right) Rucker Canyon Lake in the Chiricahuas. This tiny piece of water holds rainbow trout in an unmatched setting. David Muench

(Below) A fisherman and his chief assistant.
Dick Dietrich

(Left) A happy duck hunter. Judd Cooney

(Center, left to right) Sandhill crane. James Tallon
Breakfast for javelina. Robert Campbell
Afield with a bow. Judd Cooney

(Bottom) Mearns' quail country near Sonoita.
James Tallon

(Right) Mearns' quail are found in the high grassland hills
south and east of Tucson. They are splendid birds of the
unspoiled mountain slopes. Larry Toschik

In the Tucson Mountains, saguaro, mesquite, and
paloverde provide excellent cover for mule deer. Jerry Jacka

(Inset) Desert mule deer. James Tallon

Region 10

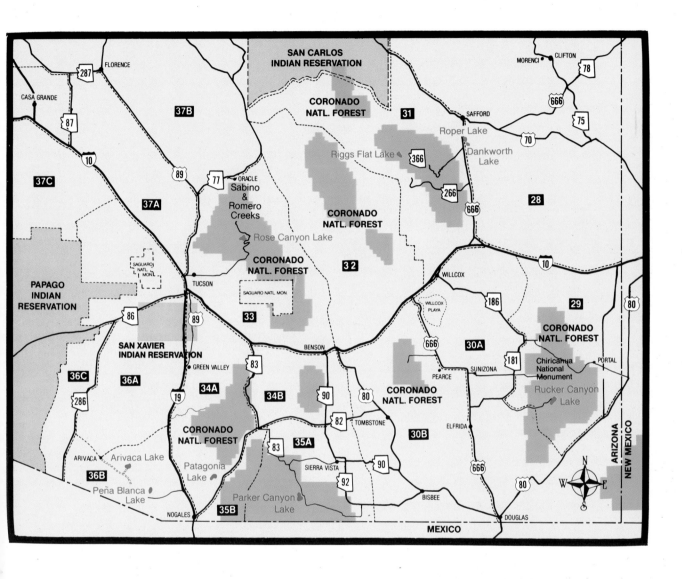

Map labels:

SAN CARLOS INDIAN RESERVATION

CLIFTON
MORENCI
287 FLORENCE
CASA GRANDE
CORONADO NATL. FOREST
87
37B
31 SAFFORD
666
10
75
89 77 ORACLE
Sabino & Romero Creeks
Riggs Flat Lake
366
Roper Lake
Dankworth Lake
70
37C
37A
266
666
CORONADO NATL. FOREST
28
SAGUARO NATL. MON.
Rose Canyon Lake
CORONADO NATL. FOREST
PAPAGO INDIAN RESERVATION
TUCSON
SAGUARO NATL. MON.
32
WILLCOX
10
80
86
89
33
WILLCOX PLAYA
186
29
SAN XAVIER INDIAN RESERVATION
GREEN VALLEY
CORONADO NATL. FOREST
30A
181
CORONADO NATL. FOREST
36C
36A
83
34A
34B
90
80
666
CORONADO NATL. FOREST
Chiricahua National Monument
PORTAL
286
19
82
TOMBSTONE
SUNIZONA
PEARCE
Rucker Canyon Lake
ARIVACA Arivaca Lake
CORONADO NATL. FOREST
35A
90
30B
ELFRIDA
ARIZONA
NEW MEXICO
36B
Patagonia Lake
83
SIERRA VISTA
92
666
80
Peña Blanca Lake
Parker Canyon Lake
NOGALES
35B
BISBEE
DOUGLAS
MEXICO

N W E S

0 5 10 20 30 40
Scale of Miles

Legend:
- Interstate Highway
- U.S. Highway
- State Highway
- 0 Game Management Unit
- National Forest
- Indian Reservation

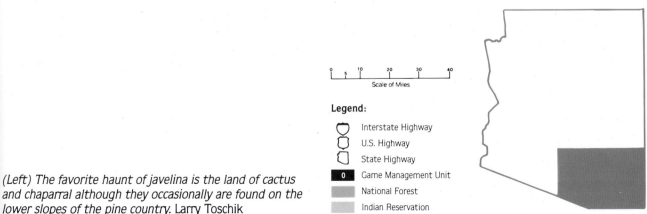

(Left) The favorite haunt of javelina is the land of cactus and chaparral although they occasionally are found on the lower slopes of the pine country. Larry Toschik

181

Fishing Southeastern Arizona

The list of fishing options is short in the sections of the state south and east of Tucson. There are a few man-made lakes—all small—and a couple of hike-in streams, also small, hardly enough to slake the fishing thirst of anglers who live in this part of Arizona. So rod-and-reel fans here tend to travel to other parts of the state for their sport: to the White Mountains for trout or the big reservoirs along the Gila and Salt rivers for bass and crappie.

The water that does exist in this region is well used. In three lakes near the Mexican border, for example, warm-water species like bass, catfish, and bluegills provide fishing targets during the spring, summer, and fall. Then, when winter cools the water and fishing for those species slows, rainbow trout are stocked.

Trout limits in these lakes with a "southern exposure" are the same as those in other parts of the state, so check regulations. The water is used from November to March for trout. When the lakes warm in the spring, the bass take over again. Most of the lakes also feature campgrounds, so visitors get a chance to double-dip and enjoy the special character of these popular reservoirs.

Peña Blanca Lake

Peña Blanca Lake is just forty-five acres, but it winds through a gentle canyon in the oak-covered hills and seems much larger. Bass, including some occasional lunkers in the eight-pound class, bite best from April to October. This also applies to channel catfish, bluegills, and crappies.

In October, the water cools, and it's harder to fill stringers with these species. Hatchery trucks ride to the rescue, however, and every month from November to March, a load of pan-size rainbows is stocked in the lake. There's always a chance of a mixed bag, though, and many a trout angler has been surprised with a big catfish that inhaled a chunk of cheese meant for a ten-inch trout.

There's a surprising variety of cover for so small a lake, with reeds, drowned trees, stumps, rock piles, and steep, rocky cliffs to prospect for finny gold. The resort at the lake offers a cafe, store, motel, and boat rentals. The Coronado National Forest boat-launch ramp is free, and a campground is available nearby. Elevation here is 4000 feet. Access is via a paved road leading about ten miles west from Interstate Route 19; take the Ruby exit about six miles north of Nogales.

Arivaca Lake

Arivaca Lake gives anglers a chance at outsize largemouth bass, channel catfish, and redear sunfish—all from a tiny lake that is only ninety acres when completely full. The lake is about ten miles southeast of the little community of the same name. Access is also possible via Peña Blanca Lake and Ruby. Either way, you're on unpaved road beyond Arivaca or Peña Blanca.

Although most of the lake's fish are average size, a bass over eleven pounds, a giant channel cat of thirty-one pounds, and redear sunfish over two pounds have been taken. The possibility of a fish that large spices up any trip to Arivaca.

There's a boat-launch ramp here—the lake is restricted to electric motors only—with parking area and restroom, but no other facilities. Shore fishing is possible, but a boat is a big help. Small craft like canoes, cartoppers, and inflatables are perfect. Fall, winter, and spring are the top times. Elevation is 3750 feet, so temperatures may get uncomfortable during the day in the summer months but are otherwise mild and delightful.

Patagonia Lake

Patagonia Lake is the area's largest at 250 surface acres. The lake is divided into two zones: one where wakeless speed is enforced, the other with no motor or speed restrictions. There is fishing for largemouth bass, crappie, flathead, channel catfish, and bluegill, with the best catches reported in spring, summer, and fall months. Rainbow trout are stocked monthly from November to March. Expert anglers take good strings of bass and crappie from Patagonia, and some big catfish come from the lake during the summer, especially for those who fish at night. Crappies are best in late winter and early spring.

There is good fish cover in the form of reed beds and drowned trees. The lake is part of the state parks system and has a campground and paved launch ramp. A concession has a store and rental boats. Access is via State Route 82 from Nogales or Patagonia, then four miles of unpaved road north to the lake. The elevation is 4000 feet.

Parker Canyon Lake

Parker Canyon Lake is the other member of the trio of lakes that receives winter stocks of pan-size rainbow trout. It puts out largemouth bass, catfish, and bluegills as well, and has a reputation as a super spot to take channel cats in the ten- to twenty-pound class. For bass, bounce plastic worms off the face of the dam or try top-water lures along the edges of weed beds.

The 5200-foot elevation here makes the winter months a bit chilly, but sunny days are the rule, and some good trout are taken as well as an occasional bass. Facilities include a resort with furnished cabins, rental boats, plus a small store. The Coronado National Forest operates the campground and offers a free launch ramp. Outboards to eight horsepower are allowed on the lake's 120 acres. The lake is thirty miles southeast of Sonoita, with the last twenty miles unpaved but suitable for any sort of vehicle.

Final note: Parker Canyon is also the home of big green sunfish, chunky, big mouthed representatives of this tribe of eager biters. A number of state record "greenies" have come from the lake, with the summer months providing most of the biggies.

Rucker Canyon Lake (Pond)

Rucker Canyon Lake is tucked away in a scenic canyon to the west of the Chiricahua Mountains northeast of Douglas. Only three acres when full, it would be too small to mention in any other part of the state, but the rainbow trout stocked here during the spring and early summer get a lot of attention. The elevation is 5700 feet, making the water too warm for trout stocking during the July-September period so catch your rainbows early.

There is a parking lot with nearby camping, but no other facilities. Boats are restricted to electric motors. Most anglers fish from shore with bait, but small spinning lures work well in Rucker's clear water. Access roads are unpaved but generally adequate for any but the largest types of recreational vehicles.

Riggs Flat Lake

Riggs Flat Lake is worth visiting just for the views along the road from Safford to the top of Mount Graham. The ten-acre lake is at 9000 feet, so snow closes the road from late fall to late spring. Rainbow trout are the mainstay and apparently some of them spend the winter, since occasional fish in the fourteen- to eighteen-inch class are taken. Facilities include a campground, launch ramp (electric motors only), and parking area. Bait is popular, but a small Z-Ray, Roostertail, or Mepps lure will catch trout, too, and often the larger fish are taken on flies or lures.

Rose Canyon Lake

Rose Canyon Lake is a good example of put-and-take fishing. It sits on the shoulder of the Santa Catalina Mountains, half an hour's drive from half a million people in the Tucson area. The lake's seven acres can't possibly grow enough trout to take care of the pressure it receives, so hatchery trucks make regular visits from May to September. The trucks from the Arizona Game and Fish Department *put* while anglers *take* the rainbow trout.

No boats are allowed, so long casts with light line and small spinning lures, or a bubble and fly setup, will let you prospect in parts of the lake not normally covered by bait fishermen. Access from Tucson is all paved. Take the Hitchcock Highway toward Mount Lemmon and watch for the Rose Canyon turnoff about two-thirds of the way up.

The Santa Catalinas

Two creeks, **Sabino** and **Romero**, are also high in the Catalina range above Tucson, and fishermen who want to try them for rainbow or brown trout will have to do some hiking first. The creeks are small, stocked only sporadically, and thus are never a sure thing. So a twelve-inch trout taken from a tiny pool gives more satisfaction than a long stringer of fish taken from some easily accessible spot. In fact, releasing that trout so it can provide sport for the next angler is a source of satisfaction for many.

Roper Lake State Park

Two lakes, **Roper** and **Dankworth**, are part of a state park just off U. S. Route 666, about four miles south of Safford. Both contain largemouth bass, channel catfish, and bluegills, and Dankworth also has some crappies in residence. Elevation here is 3000 feet, and most fishing is done in the spring and fall months to avoid the warm summer days. Boats on thirty-acre Roper and ten-acre Dankworth are restricted to electric motors. Bass fishermen pick up some largemouths at both lakes, but channel cats are the main item, along with the abundant but usually small bluegills. Try flies or small poppers for bluegills at Dankworth, especially in the shade of shoreline trees or along the banks of reeds. There are picnic areas and a restroom at Dankworth, and a campground and launch ramp at Roper.

Peña Blanca Lake. J. Peter Mortimer

Hunting Southeastern Arizona

This region has some of the best features of other parts of the state, and it mixes in some of its own. The result is an unusual landscape: vistas of gently rolling grassland punctuated by sharply upthrust mountain ranges, sky islands rising above a sea of green and gold. And as the ridges slope upward, they are dotted with oak, then piñon and juniper, and finally the big pines, fir, spruce, and aspen.

This ascent from high desert to alpine conditions represents a number of life zones, each with its significant flora and fauna. The diversity of habitat is reflected in the relative abundance of game.

Deer Hunting

There are two species here, the **mule deer** and the **Coues whitetail.** Their habitats do overlap, but generally where you find one species, you will not find the other. The whitetail is a small deer. A mature buck may weigh no more than one hundred pounds, and its antlers are correspondingly tiny. But what it lacks in size is made up in brains, and many hunters consider a trophy-size Coues deer one of the ultimate challenges in Arizona hunting. (The name should be pronounced "cows" after the Army surgeon who first classified the deer, but is widely mispronounced as "coos.")

Hunts in this section of the state sometimes call for any antlered deer but are most often for either mule deer or whitetail. Generally, mule-deer hunting is best in the lower elevations of the units along the eastern border: 28, 29, 30, and 31. Best whitetail success figures are from these same units, plus 35 and 36. The whitetail hunt is divided into two segments, one in November and the later season in December, and this latter hunt accounts for some of the best deer hunting in the state.

The mule deer generally inhabit the lower parts of the mountain islands, the whitetails the higher country. However, many Coues deer come from the rolling oak-grassland ridges that characterize some of the low land between the high ranges. The whitetail seasons include most of the units in the southeastern corner of the state, so hunters are not restricted to a certain area. The late hunt occurs during the rut or breeding season, and the usually wily bucks tend to lose a bit of caution. Most whitetail units on the late hunt exceed the statewide success average that hovers somewhere in the low twenties, and the best have percentages in the thirties and forties with occasional rates even higher. Whether you bring home venison or not, you're hunting for a unique species in beautiful country during generally good weather, and that's a triple order of satisfaction.

Antelope Hunting

Small herds of antelope dwell in the San Rafael and Sulphur Spring valleys, and limited hunts are held each fall. Antelope numbers are limited by available habitat and by gradually encroaching civilization. Some transplants to new areas have been made in recent years. Units 31 and 32 have one hunt; 35A and 35B have the other.

Turkey Hunting

Turkeys are found in a number of the mountain ranges in this region, and both spring (gobbler) and fall hunts are held. The spring season is by permit only, and Units 29, 33, and 34A are involved. Like turkey hunts in other parts of the state, success is relatively low—on the order of ten to fifteen percent. The fall hunt is limited to Unit 33—the Santa Catalina Mountains just north of Tucson. The higher reaches of the Catalinas are rugged and hard to hunt, and not many gun-toters take advantage of the season. Recent surveys show fewer than two dozen birds have been taken each year.

Bear and Lion Hunting

Very few bears are taken in this region, and Units 29, 31 and 32 are generally the only ones open on the fall hunt. The Pinaleno Mountains, (better known as Mount Graham) in Unit 31 are the top spot. Limited permit hunts (drawing) are authorized in some units during the spring. Some small populations may occur in other mountain ranges.

The rugged mountains in the far southeastern corner of the state are among the top lion spots in Arizona. Recent surveys estimate twenty to twenty-five animals taken each year. The great majority are collected by hunters using dogs. Units 28, 30, and 35 provide the majority of the lions, and the months from October to March are most popular.

Javelina Hunting

The javelina or collared peccary is the northernmost member of a family that lives in South and Central America. The javelina weighs less than fifty pounds on the average, is not aggressive, and will not make an unprovoked charge. Its nose is super-keen and it can hear okay, too. But it cannot see well, and that makes it very stalkable. The meat is more like rabbit than pork and is very good if properly cared for in the field.

This is prime javelina country. Though the little desert porkers are found as far north as Prescott and the Mogollon Rim, the mesquite and oak grassland of this region accounts for about three-fourths of the 20,000-plus permits authorized each year.

The entire region is open to archery javelina hunting every January, and the diminutive peccary is the perfect target for bow hunters. If you're very careful—and a bit lucky—it's possible to stalk within a few yards of a herd of javelina, and bow hunters often measure shots in feet rather than yards.

Hunting

ow hunters enjoy nearly the same success as the firearms nters, with twenty to twenty-five percent bringing home trophy.

Units 36 and 37 tend to be a bit below the statewide ccess average; all the other units in this region equal or ceed those figures. Units 28, 29, and 30 usually provide e best javelina hunting in the state. Because the animals e a relatively long way from the population centers of oenix and Tucson, the odds of getting drawn for a permit e excellent.

Most javelinas are found in the foothills of the mountain nges or in the rolling oak-mesquite grassland between the nges. Most hunters simply walk through the country, pping to spot one of the animals. But sitting on a ridge and sing binoculars saves wear and tear on boot soles and sually means more targets, too. The season is in late bruary and early March.

Small-Game Hunting

There's some good hunting for both **mourning** and **hitewing doves** during the early part of the September ason in the areas north and west of Tucson, in the farming eas around Willcox, and from Coolidge and Casa Grande uth and east. Cropland and orchards draw the birds in all ese localities.

There's also some good shooting around some of the sert water holes early and late in the day as birds come in water or roost. The farmland along the Gila at Safford is a od bet, too. Most of the brush and trees along rivers in is region have been cleared in the name of flood control or plant crops, so the historic nesting areas that produced ns of thousands of doves in past years are gone.

This, in combination with the trend to plant cotton ther than grain crops, means the numbers of doves pres-t in the 1950s and '60s will probably never be seen again. owever, those populations were unnaturally high, so old-mers tend to write off present-day hunting as hardly orth the bother. But shotgunners in other parts of the untry envy us our sport, and many travel here just to hunt ves.

This region contains three species of **quail: Gambel's, aled,** and **Mearns'.** The familiar top-knotted Gambel's ail are found in the lower desert, with the best popula-ons in the area from Tucson north to Winkelman and orence Junction, south to Florence and Casa Grande, and ck to Tucson. The Willcox area has good Gambel's hunt-g, and so does some of the lower country between Willcox d Douglas as well as farmland and foothills around afford.

Scaled quail occasionally are found in the same country as ambel's; in fact they sometimes hybridize, but generally e scaleys are most prevalent in the southeastern corner of is region, along both sides of a line between Willcox and

Douglas. The foothills of most of the mountains south of Tucson and east of the Papago Indian Reservation also have some good scaled quail populations. Scaleys tend to run, just as their cousins the Gambel's do, but if you can find a covey in decent ground cover, they will sit tight.

The Mearns' quail are creatures of the oak-grassland areas. They are found in the higher elevations of many of the ranges in this region, but the best populations exist within the rough rectangle formed by Interstate Route 10 from Tucson to Benson, U. S. Route 80 to Bisbee, the U. S.-Mexico border to Nogales, and Interstate 19 back to Tucson.

Coveys are small family groups of six to eight, and they forage for food on the grassy hillsides, almost always in scattered oak groves. Unlike the other Arizona quail, which depend on seeds for the bulk of their diet, Mearns' quail are equipped with long claws on their feet, and they scratch and dig for the tender tuberous roots of grasses.

"Fool's quail" is an old nickname for the Mearns'. It refers to their habit of sitting very still and letting danger pass close by, rather than flushing and flying. You can spend a lot of time walking in Mearns' quail country without seeing them, so a good pointing dog is as important as your shotgun. The birds hold very tight, and you can walk in ahead of the dog on point and literally kick out the quail.

Mearns' quail nest later in the year than other kinds of quail in our state, so the season opens in late November. Nesting success is closely tied to the amount and timing of summer rains, and populations can fluctuate sharply from year to year.

Bandtail pigeons are pursued by relatively few hunters in this region. The Chiricahua, Huachuca, Santa Rita, Cata-lina, and Pinaleno ranges get most of the pressure, with the Mount Graham area best. Look for **cottontails** along desert washes, around water holes, and in the desert close to farmland.

Waterfowl hunting is mostly on water holes and is best late in the season. There's hunting for both **ducks** and **geese** along the Gila River up- and downstream from Saf-ford. The farmlands around Willcox are another popular waterfowl spot, and it's here that a limited hunt for **sandhill cranes** is held each fall. The big birds gather at Willcox Playa, the marshy bed of an ancient lake, and fly out to feed on crops in the area. Only a few dozen cranes are taken each year.

Squirrel hunting in this region is more or less confined to the Catalinas in Unit 33 and the Pinalenos (Mount Graham) in Unit 31. Most are Abert squirrels, although a few Arizona gray squirrels are also present in the Catalinas. The Santa Rita, Chiricahua, and Huachuca ranges are closed to squirrel hunting. Look for Aberts in open ponderosa pine forests and the grays in oak-walnut country five thousand to six thou-sand feet in elevation, especially along stream beds with good tree canopies.

185

Flies custom tied by Lon Ellington

Muddler Minnow

Goddard Caddis

Lon's Damsel Nymph

Pheasant Wing Hopper

Lon's Bass Bug

Black Woolly Becker Lake Special

Mepps

Z-Ray

Rapala 9s

Flat Fish

Dardevle Spoon

Rapala Fat Rap

Plastic Worms

Fishing and Hunting Tips

Fishing Striped Bass

Striped bass are school fish: Where you find one, you'll find others. The exception is during the May-June spawning period, when larger females may be alone.

Threadfin shad are the number-one staple for striped bass in all Arizona lakes, but they also relish crayfish. Troll or cast shiny, shad-imitating plugs or spoons.

Unlike other bass, the striper does not build a nest. The female broadcasts her eggs, and they are fertilized by attendant males. The eggs are semibuoyant and float for the two or three days it takes them to hatch. Mortality is high, so females are prolific. A forty-pounder may lay up to five million eggs.

Generally, stripers follow threadfin shad, and they are deep during the winter months, shallow in the summertime. September and October are months when the shad are close to the surface, and "boils" occur as schools of striped bass herd huge numbers of shad to the surface and feed on them. Anything shiny thrown into the melee means an instant strike.

The largest fish are always females. The freshwater world record was taken from the Colorado River between Mohave and Havasu lakes in 1977. It weighed fifty-nine pounds, twelve ounces.

Striped bass helped the Plymouth colony to survive its first winter, and a permit to fish stripers commercially was one of the first documents ever issued in America.

Fishing Largemouth Bass

Threadfin shad, again, are the top attraction for Arizona largemouth bass, but the larger specimens seem to prefer crayfish. Bass weighing more than five pounds invariably have their stomachs full of the mini-lobsters, usually called crawdads by anglers.

Wobbling, diving lures, often lumped together under the name "crankbaits," are a good bet for bass when the fish are in water shallower than fifteen feet. There are dozens of brands and models, but look for shiny, shad-imitating finishes in plugs like the Spot, Deep Wee R, Bayou Boogie, Killer B-II, Wiggle Wart, Double Deep Shad, Shadrap, and similar versions.

Any bass over three pounds is a "good" fish. The state record, taken from Roosevelt Lake in 1956, weighed fourteen pounds, two ounces. The odds are long on any bass over ten pounds, but the best lakes to look for that lunker are Saguaro, Canyon, San Carlos, and Alamo—in no particular order of preference.

Plastic worms may be the best lure ever invented to fool bass. Use the four- to six-inch worm in purple, black, brown, blue, or bright red. Models with "firetails" or curly tails are okay, too. Fish them right on the bottom, and move them very slowly.

Begin your bassing day by fishing shallow—right up on the shoreline in one to two feet of water. Then gradually move out, changing lures and techniques until you find the fish. They may be in water as deep as fifty to sixty feet or more, but most of the time you'll find them somewhere in water shallower than twenty-five feet.

Fishing Trout with Bait

Live worms—garden hackle, fly fishermen call 'em—probably catch more Arizona trout than all other methods combined, but salmon eggs, whole-kernel corn, cheese, and bite-size marshmallows (and sometimes a combination of two or more of these) also fool a lot of fish.

You'll catch more trout if you use light leader. The last three or four feet of your line should be monofilament no heavier than four-pound test, but two-pound test will catch more fish. If you set the reel's drag properly, you can land a big fish on light line. The state-record rainbow, a twenty-one pounder, was caught on six-pound line.

Be sure you cover the hook completely (including the eye) with whatever bait you use. Trout can spot immediately anything that looks unnatural, particularly in the clear water of small streams.

Avoid adding weight on your line, if possible. If you must add sinkers to cast properly, begin with a light split shot and add more weight only if needed. When a trout picks up your bait and begins to move, even the slight drag of a small split shot may cause it to spit the hook back out.

Use the least amount of bait necessary to cover the hook. Trout have dainty appetites, so big chunks of bait may just be ignored.

You may catch a small trout and choose to release it. If it is hooked deeply, don't risk injuring the fish; simply cut the leader and release the trout. The hook will rust out within a few days, and in the meantime it will not bother the trout's feeding.

Fishing Trout with Lures and Flies

It is important to vary the speed of your retrieve when casting lures. Some days, the trout seem to prefer the spoon or spinner to be zipping along through the water, but a slow, erratic retrieve, with the lure just off the bottom, is more often the best bet. Do some experimenting.

The wooly-worm family of flies imitate a wide variety of buggy creatures, and for beginning fly fishermen, a handful of brown, black, or green wooly worms is a good way to be sure a fish will inhale your offering.

Trolling a spoon or spinner—something like the Z-Ray, Mepps, Roostertail, or Panther-Martin—is an excellent way to prospect for trout in a lake. Adjust the depth the lure is running by letting out more line. If you're not hooking the bottom occasionally, chances are you won't be hooking many fish, either.

The heat of the summer sun often produces a late-afternoon hatch of insects on Arizona high-country trout lakes. Occasionally, the trout are maddeningly specific about what fly pattern they will take, but generally you can get some great action with any size twelve or fourteen well-dressed fly.

The ideal Arizona vest-pocket tackle box: one eighth-ounce Z-Ray in chrome, one small Panther-Martin in yellow, one small Roostertail in black, one brown wooly worm, one black wooly worm, and one peacock lady—all in size twelve.

Insects make up more than four-fifths of a trout's diet, but fish over fourteen inches in length tend to be cannibalistic, so offer them larger flies and lures that appeal to their heightened appetites.

Hunting Deer

Given good water and cover, deer are creatures of habit. They will browse on a certain hillside, go to water at a certain place and time, and use the same patch of country as a nighttime resting place. If undisturbed by human encroachment or weather, their daily timetables are very predictable.

Bucks and does live apart except during the late fall-early winter breeding season. However, small bucks, spikes or two-points that are last year's fawns, may stay with the does through their second fall, then take off on their own.

Acorns are the steak and lobster of the deer menu. If there are oaks in the area and there's been a good acorn crop, look for deer in the vicinity.

Recent studies show deer do not feed at night as much as some claim. They do prefer very early and very late hours, so be in position to hunt before first light and plan to stay afield during the last hour of the day.

To preserve deer hides in warm fall weather, scrape as much meat as possible from the skin, salt liberally, and roll with the hair side in. Keep it cool, and do not put in a plastic bag. If you're planning on a trophy mount, check with your taxidermist for instructions before the hunt.

Most deer are shot at ranges of less than one hundred yards. Sight in rifles of .243, .308, .270, and 30:06 calibers to shoot two inches high at one hundred yards. They'll be "on" for as far as most hunters can shoot accurately.

Whitetail deer and javelina often are found in the same areas, and their tracks are similar. Whitetail tracks have sharper points, and javelinas' tend to be rounded or heart-shaped. Deer droppings resemble blackened beans, and those of javelina resemble a domestic hog's.

Hunting Elk

Arizona elk begin their breeding season in September. Each mature bull rounds up a harem of cows that he jealously guards from other males. During this period, it's possible to use an artificial call to locate or attract a bull.

Elk originally were plains animals, and they generally graze on grass rather than browse on the tips of brush or trees as do deer. They have moved to the timbered sections of the state in response to the pressures of civilization.

Early and late hours of the day are best for elk hunters. The animals may disappear from forest openings soon after the first hint of daylight, so it's important to be in position while it's still black-dark.

Given a choice, elk prefer to spend the day in thick cover, such as jack-pine thickets, dense blowdowns, or aspen draws, especially if the cover is on a hillside so that rising air can carry scent to the bedded animals.

A mature bull can weigh upwards of 1000 pounds, and its hide acts as a thick insulating blanket. It's important to skin the animal quickly and to keep the meat cool until it can be processed.

Though many elk spend the summer and fall months at elevations of 8000 to 10,000 feet, others live year-round in juniper-grassland areas. Large, grassy meadows in timber country are obvious elk-hunting spots, but don't ignore smaller openings or those made by man, including log roads and power-line rights of way.

Hunting Quail

Quail, like many other wild creatures, feed early and late in the day. Gambel's and scaled quail roost in trees and are up at dawn. Mearns' quail sleep on the ground, and they tend to stay put until the sun is up. All three species feed, rest during midday hours, then feed again in the afternoon before retiring.

It helps to learn some quail "language." They have a wide range of calls, chirps, and clucks. The Gambel's have a re-assemble call that is distinctive, and if you break up a covey, it's often possible to pinpoint individual birds by listening for the call. You can use an artificial call to find birds, too. If you sound off and there are birds in the area, you'll usually get a response.

Mearns' quail are equipped with long, pointed claws. They use them to dig up grass roots and tubers, and when a covey, usually about eight birds, finishes a feeding session, it's easy to spot the results: It appears as if a herd of javelina have been digging in the area. Look for sign on grassy hillsides, beneath oak trees, and in small draws that lead to deeper canyons.

Gambel's quail hunters sometimes have to make a choice. Coveys during the early part of the season are small — usually eight to fifteen birds — but many of them are the young and thus easier to hunt. By the December-January period, smaller coveys merge, and groups of fifty to one hundred birds are not unusual. But these birds are adults and very tough to hunt.

Tips

Mearns' quail sit so tight in cover that they're nearly impossible to hunt without a good dog. And although Gambel's and scaled quail tend to run, if you find decent ground cover and can break up the covey, the singles and doubles will hold for a dog very well. Using a dog — for whatever species — also means few, if any, lost birds.

Shotguns with open bores take more birds. Many experts use skeet or improved-cylinder barrels year-round. A modified choke may be necessary late in the season when longer shots are the rule, but a full choke is an unnecessary handicap anytime.

Hunting Javelina

The javelina, also known as the collared peccary, is a small, mild-mannered animal averaging thirty-two or thirty-three pounds, field dressed. In spite of stories to the contrary, authorities have been unable to authenticate a single instance of this so-called wild pig's ever charging a human.

Arizona is the northern limit of the javelina's range, but the animals seem to be slowly working their way northward in our state. They are now seen frequently in the Prescott area and just below the Mogollon Rim. The best places to find javelina remain the desert areas of the southeastern corner of the state, the foothills of the mountains in the central portion, and the lower elevations of the San Carlos and Fort Apache reservations.

Sometimes called "musk hogs," javelina have a scent gland that emits a powerful, skunklike odor. It looks like a second navel and appears on the middle of the animal's back, about six inches up from the vestigial tail. It is a skin gland, and when the javelina's hide is removed, the gland comes with it. There's no need to remove it ahead of time and thus ruin what can be fine, tough leather made from the hide.

The javelina has an excellent nose and at least good hearing, but it is cursed with lousy eyesight. For this reason, it is comparatively easy to stalk, and archers often measure their shots in feet rather than yards. Take your time, get the wind in your favor, move slowly, and there's no reason you can't get up close.

A herd of javelina — properly called a sounder — averages eight to ten animals, but groups of twenty are not unusual. Javelina have a home range of about one to two square miles — lots of country in Arizona's up-and-down desert — so they are sometimes very difficult to find.

Javelina arise when the sun is well up, feed until late morning, nap, feed again, then retire. They relish roots, tubers, and the fresh, green growth that follows winter and spring rains. Agave, prickly pear, and other cactus are also on the grocery list, as are acorns, berries, and cactus fruit.

Hunting Turkey

The turkey is an American bird, unknown in Europe until the Spaniards arrived in Mexico in the early 1500s and took a few samples back home. Most of the new, exotic spices, foods, and fabrics were coming from the East in those days, and somehow the word got out that these strange-looking birds had come from Turkey.

Turkeys fly from their roost tree at dawn, feed during the morning, then seek a spot to dust and rest until late afternoon, when they feed back toward the roost.

Best bet to ambush a turkey: Stake out a water hole. If you see tracks and other signs indicating recent use of a water source, build a blind and wait. It's not very exciting, but chances are the birds will show some time during a two-or three-day period.

When it comes to meals, turkeys are opportunists. They eat insects, berries, seeds, tubers, and new, green growth. They also relish acorns: One bird ate 221 acorns in a single session.

If your last wild turkey tended to be tough, it may have been an old bird. They can live for a dozen years and weigh as much as thirty-five pounds, although any over twenty pounds is a very big wild turkey.

Arizona has a population of about 20,000 turkeys, making it one of the top half-dozen turkey states in the country. Not many are taken each year — an indication that turkeys in general and gobblers in particular are among the wiliest of all wild creatures.

Hunting Bighorn Sheep

If you apply for a sheep permit in some of the more popular areas, you could face odds of up to one to two-hundred to one. That means that if you do get drawn, it's important to get out and scout your area ahead of the hunt. Then you can spend the two weeks of the season looking for the best ram on the mountain, rather than looking for a sheep of any kind.

Sheep distribution depends on the availability of water, so check water holes and seeps for sign and tracks.

Success is high on Arizona sheep hunts, probably because of the commitment made by those who draw the precious permits. Most hunters spend half a dozen or more weekends scouting and plan on staying in the field for the entire season, if that much time is needed. Wise hunters spend time getting in top physical shape, too.

A good spotting scope and quality binoculars are nearly as important to a sheep hunter as the rifle. So is learning how to use the scope and binocs.

One of the best ways a permit holder can help ensure success on his hunt is to attend the free sheep-hunting clinic offered each fall by the Arizona Desert Bighorn Sheep Society. The hunter will see slide shows and movies and hear talks on all aspects of the desert bighorn.

Index

Index